The Kings and Their Gods

THE KINGS AND THEIR GODS

The Pathology of Power

Daniel Berrigan

WILLIAM B. EERDMANS PUBLISHING COMPANY
GRAND RAPIDS, MICHIGAN / CAMBRIDGE, U.K.

© 2008 Daniel Berrigan

All rights reserved

Wm. B. Eerdmans Publishing Co.

2140 Oak Industrial Drive N.E., Grand Rapids, Michigan 49505 /
P.O. Box 163, Cambridge CB3 9PU U.K.

Printed in the United States of America

13 12 11 10 09 08   7 6 5 4 3 2 1

Library of Congress Cataloging-in-Publication Data

Berrigan, Daniel.
The kings and their gods: the pathology of power / Daniel Berrigan.
p.   cm.
Includes bibliographical references.
ISBN 978-0-8028-6043-9 (pbk.: alk. paper)
1. Bible. O.T. Kings — Commentaries.   I. Title.

BS1335.53.B47   2008
222'.507 — dc22

2007044807

www.eerdmans.com

A Note on the Use of Scripture in This Volume

The basic structure of this text follows the chapter-and-verse structure of 1 and 2 Kings in the NRSV. In the text, Berrigan occasionally uses quotations (sometimes slightly altered) from the NRSV. More often he uses quotations (sometimes slightly altered) from the NAB. And sometimes he is rendering the biblical text in his own poetic equivalent, or creating a rich interplay of different biblical versions.

Chapter-and-verse citations have been used infrequently in the text to keep it as free from technical apparatus as possible.

Those quotations from the New Revised Standard Version of the Bible are copyright © 1989 by the Division of Christian Education of the National Council of Churches of Christ in the U.S.A., and used by permission.

Those quotations from the New American Bible with Revised New Testament and Revised Psalms are copyright © 1991, 1986, 1970 by the Confraternity of Christian Doctrine, Washington, D.C. and are used by permission of the copyright owner. All rights reserved.

Acknowledgments

The author and publisher gratefully acknowledge permission to reprint the following materials:

W. H. Auden. "Epitaph on a Tyrant," copyright © 1940 and renewed 1968 by W. H. Auden, from *Collected Poems* by W. H. Auden. Used by permission of Random House, Inc.

Faiz Ahmed Faiz. "The Tyrant," in *The True Subject*, copyright © 1987 by Princeton University Press. Reprinted by permission of Princeton University Press.

Czeslaw Milosz. "A Nation," from *The Collected Poems: 1931-1987* by Czeslaw Milosz. Copyright © 1988 by Czeslaw Milosz Royalties, Inc. Reprinted by permission of HarperCollins Publishers.

Czeslaw Milosz. "A Task," from *The Collected Poems: 1931-1987* by Czeslaw Milosz. Copyright © 1988 by Czeslaw Milosz Royalties, Inc. Reprinted by permission of HarperCollins Publishers.

Howard Nemerov. "Ultima Ratio Reagan." Reprinted by permission of Margaret Nemerov.

Rainer Maria Rilke. "Ich lese es heraus aus deinem Wort / I read it here in your very word," from *Book of Hours: Love Poems to God* by Rainer Maria Rilke, translated by Anita Barrows and Joanna Macy, copyright © 1996 by Anita Barrows and Joanna Macy. Used by permission of Riverhead Books, an imprint of Penguin Group (USA) Inc.

R. S. Thomas. "Waiting," from *Collected Poems: 1945-1990* by R. S. Thomas. Reprinted by permission of Orion Publishing Group.

Georg Trakl. "In the East," in *Autumn Sonata* by Georg Trakl, translated by Daniel Simko. Reprinted by permission of Moyer Bell, Ltd.

Contents

Contents

Introduction

"And why do you pray, Mosche?" I asked him.
*   "I pray to the God within me that He will give me the strength to ask Him the right questions."*

Elie Wiesel, Night

Tradition has honored the books of Judges, Samuel, Kings, and Maccabees as "religious" or "biblical" or "divinely inspired" history. Puzzling indeed.

A question has lingered for centuries. What instruction from Yahweh may be conveyed in these accounts, steeped as they are in mayhem, slaughter, betrayal, intrigue, and bravado; rife as they are with fractious sons and foolish fathers, brothers betraying and killing brothers, women deprived of status and dignity, predatory enmities periodically erupting, and wars breeding wars that breed wars?

"Religious history," this brimstone brew?

~

Only a minuscule portion of the books could be deemed edifying. Few ideal humans emerge from among the kings and generals and counselors; few in the teeming "schools" of prophets.

A further question, the most grievous and puzzling of all: What to make of the Yahweh of these stories, a being who in no way disapproves of vile behavior, is inclined rather to bless it, to account moral delinquents his "chosen," and with prodding from on high, to urge base instincts into action?

What then of "divinely inspired" history? Why are blood-ridden pages uniquely honored in church and synagogue, honored under the blessed cope of "Word of God" — so entitled, along with the stories and teachings of sublime prophets, martyrs, and truth tellers?

~

To speak of Christians, can our God incarnate in Jesus be one with this Yahweh, a deity of kings and their wars, enthroned in a cloud of moral ambiguity, implicated in wickedness trumpeted as virtue?

Let us stand back from the stories and venture a suggestion. The books of Judges, Samuel, Kings, and Maccabees imply that we humans must move in great darkness before we are blessed and enter the light. This, it would seem, is the law of the Fall. We must undergo the anti-human, the inhuman enthroned, wielding life-and-death authority. Behold the ancestry from which we spring, we children of primal catastrophe. Let us ponder such forebears, and weep.

We must suffer the anti-human as well in ourselves. Here and now. The warriors, tricksters, and betrayers are not only our ancestors; they are ourselves, our present awful authorities, our likely progeny and descendants. The wars of the Kings are our wars today — these awful days of the wars in Afghanistan, Iraq, Lebanon, Darfur.

Tears, then, for the victims, and for our unredeemed selves. Tears, before we are enabled to cry out in redemptive longing, "O grant us a life that merits the name human!"

All in due time. Within our timetable, whether marked by despair or the hope that hopes on.

~

But first, it would seem, we must undergo a harsh, even shaming pedagogy. Through these books, we must come to know the worst of our ancestry — as well as the worst that lurks in ourselves. We must come to know also the truth of structures and systems, throughout the ages and today. To know that even those approved by popular opinion and attested as winning divine approval — that such, given time, swamp grace and claim, like kings of a jungle, the spoils.

We are to know that rulers are not the more virtuous for being powerful. (As if we did not know it, as if it were not a fact of our horrendous years and the military rush toward oblivion.)

And what of ourselves, the governed? We too dwell in moral darkness, deep and often unapprehended; we who approve such rulers or are prudently silent in face of their crimes. We who offer, in our secret longings, small relief from theirs. Tendencies in leader and follower are often alike, and hold firm: self-interest, ego, lust, greed, duplicity, the common mire from which spring the wily and witless among us.

And all unlikely, saints and martyrs as well.

~

In such a spirit, we are urged to ponder these books of the Kings, are invited to dwell on hardly attractive matters — our common ancestry and plight. In those pages, willy-nilly we enter a scene of recognition. We see ourselves, Americans; we witness our own behavior in the world. Behavior that is for the most part shameful.

Do our leaders differ, in any large degree, from the rulers of old? They are hardly different at all. Today too they create an economic divide of riches and rags, systems of stigma and exclusion, of racism and sexism. And endless wars, incursions, bombings, sanctions.

~

Let it be said plain. The era of the Kings is cursed of God — of true God, I mean.

The god of the kings, we are told, curses the enemies of the kings. But does not the god also curse his own, including the great kings? The curse is inferred — and the inference left to us.

The curse takes these forms, among others: a moral void, the truth of human life denied — or derided. And (surely a related matter) the all but total absence of prophets.

The few who raise voice against royal misbehavior must be accounted feeble forerunners. Generally, these pre-prophets speak ambiguously, or remain silent, colluding with the crimes of their patrons.

~

Let us pause in wonderment as the kings contrive an image of their god. They make of the deity a kind of glorified ventriloquist's dummy, placing in his mouth words by turns cunning, ferocious, calamitous, and vengeful, words that proceed from the darkness of their own hearts.

~

Let us look long, and lament the implications that lie half-revealed in the ancient story. Unsavory, relentless is this tale of us humans, ever so slowly and painfully emerging into the light. What a difficult birth, millennia long!

And bearing what into the world, in this our millennium? A social monster, yet another voracious empire?

An honest totting up of the crimes of our nation, in our lifetime, raises such questions. A torment, and yet a strange relief. The relief of recognition and confession.

~

Let it be confessed. Despite the strong interventions of the prophets (and, as Christians believe, One Intervention surpassing all others), the books of the Kings stand like a record of our own benighted century, bloody as beef newly drawn and hung.

In essentials and main driving forces, the account here set down is being enacted before our eyes. Thus the meaning behind the text.

The meaning, the warning, escapes the attention of most — including most scholars. Nonetheless, let it be said plain, even unto ennui. The system that fuels our world coincides with, even surpasses, the crimes — social, military, economic (and yes, religious) — recorded of the Kings.

It is as though we opened a Book of Kells and found there — in caricature, to be sure — our own faces. Among the demons and gargoyles and maidens and kings and spooks and monks, the sad and solitary, the gaping, concupiscent mouths — and among the angels as well. Like it or not, confess it or not, we behold in these books of the high and mighty our ancestry. And ourselves.

~

The compassion of the Word of God is thus revealed. A strange compassion, seemingly devoid of mercy. The method is irony, truth concealed in paradox, all the more striking for being masked. Hidden, often humiliated and put to scorn, the Divine awaits the mindful.

The Bible measures the mystery out; "a time, double time, half a time."

And let it also be said: the god of the Kings shockingly resembles the Baals. Like them, a deity of the realm of death, the realm of the Fall.

~

The Kings seek the divine, to a point. Who the search leads them to is another matter. They come on their god in a distorting mirror, reflecting back their own moral vagaries. Flash, flash back. A god in accord with whim, vaulting ego, profitless violence, peevish morbidity, at times a peevish resentment, a stroke of vengeance.

No prophets, as yet.

In these pages, how rare is the true and integral and tested, the man or woman of virtue, the saint. And when such a one shows face (often a woman, uncelebrated and unnamed), her fate is sure: she is ignored or crushed.

~

Let a prayer arise out of the void opened by these pages:

> Grant us knowledge of our crimes. Help us take our true bearings in the world, to confess how rarely, in public life and private, in religion and statecraft, in temple and marketplace and home — how rarely authority is joined with virtue. Grant us knowledge of our plight, that we may cry out for relief, and be drawn forth.

~

In these historical accounts, I suggest that the Bible is in the process of "deconstructing" itself. Ironically, the Word of God acts like a fiery lens, placing the empire under scrutiny.

Thus the biblical method: let the kings wage wars; let them worship an approving deity lodged in a stupendous temple (the first "National Cathedral"?). Let them join religious sacrifice and battle, legitimating, even sacralizing plain slaughter. And in this imbroglio let them drown the eye in pieties. Allow them all this. The Word of God — audacious, subversive.

~

Believers are to act as judges, prophets. Deuteronomists, if you will. Jews who take Torah seriously; Christians who take Jesus seriously. Who summon the law (love of God and the neighbor) to judge violators of the law.

When this occurs, the Word emerges from the page as rebuke and judgment. The Spirit who breathes upon the Word breathes likewise upon the believer. We pause and grow thoughtful. A tale of wickedness, whether ancient or contemporary, is imputed for what it is — wicked.

~

In these pages, the "human," as defined and enacted by those in lofty places, often proves profoundly inhuman. In the warrior, diplomat, magician, court prophet, scribe, we see deception, betrayal, alienation, blind obedience, military and diplomatic chicanery, the will to multiply victims and lay waste the earth — these lauded and puffed, seldom renounced.

~

Open the Bible, then. Let the believing community see there the worst. More, see the worst presented as noble, virtuous, raised aloft in honor. And let conclusions be drawn — based on a later tradition, nobler icons, the prophets, Christ on the cross.

Out of darkness, light. But not yet.

~

In sum, we are offered in the books of Judges, Samuel, Kings, and Maccabees a diagnosis of the pathology of power. Thus is implied a biblical anthropology, a biblical version of the human, conveyed in a stark "via negativa."

~

To our books of Kings, then.

We note that Solomon reigned 960-922 C.E., and the first edition of these books was issued around 561. Undoubtedly, in the final version of our story, many cards are wild; a complicated mix of sources and redactions rests in our hands.

And for that, the tales are all the more intriguing, one thinks.

～

The books of Kings, as they reach us, are also a prime example of "theology from above." The final editor, an undoubted genius, sounds the imperial note like a trumpet blast. Triumphalism, invincibility, sway and glory, a sense of "Behold and rejoice — here, now, the ideal, sole, irrefutable, unique ruler and system."

～

A moral code is promulgated by the god. And we are struck by the narrow scope of "the law and commandments" set down. Still, a clue lies there; the poverty of moral understanding can be laid to the absence of a far different formula: "the law and the prophets." Prophecy speaking loud and clear, interpreting, warning and blessing, praising goodness and denouncing evil in high places and low.

Nothing of this graces our books. As yet no "ruah," breath, warmth, life.

Of prime import are other matters: temple observances, liturgical etiquette, gestures of conciliation offered the god. And hardly a word reproves social injustice, slavery, crushing taxation, forced labor, a vast military machine. In matters of royal behavior, moral leeway is the rule of thumb. Greed, betrayal of friendship, assassination, war-making, degradation of women. Nothing of these is called to account, nothing so much as accounted criminal.

～

All these lapses, omissions, lunacies even. Nonetheless, as we have suggested, the texts imply a judgment. One ventures that the judgment is intentional. The medium itself is the message.

~

Eventually, overt judgment will come to bear. Prophets will offer a saving midrash. They will denounce the ambiguities and crimes of high culture, raising a cry "over against." Isaiah, Jeremiah, Ezekiel, Daniel — withstanding the worst, they raise a fierce protest against the otherwise unaccountable Kings.

And another gift of these noble spirits. Through them the moral physiognomy of the Holy stands clear. God is advocate of the "widows and orphans and the strangers in your midst."

Still, "My ways are not your ways." The prophetic word confronts an absurd claim: that the behavior of a Solomon dovetails with the divine will. No. God is the utterly Other. Let no mortal presume to stand outside judgment.

~

A Nation

. . . Pitiless to its widows and orphans, pitiless to its old people,
Stealing a crust of bread from a child's hand.

Ready to offer their lives to draw Heaven's wrath on their foes,
Smiting their enemy with the screams of orphans and women.

Entrusting power to men with the eyes of traders in gold,
Elevating men with the conscience of brothel-keepers.

The best of its sons remain unknown,
They appear once only, to die on the barricades.

. . . Great nation, invincible nation, ironic nation.
They know how to distinguish truth and yet to keep silent.

They camp on marketplaces, conversing in wisecracks,
They deal in old door handles stolen from ruins.

. . . A man of that nation, standing by his son's cradle,
Repeats words of hope, always, till now, in vain.

Czeslaw Milosz

~

Today. The Word of God is spoken for the sake of today, for us. If not, it lies dead on the page. Lift the Word from the page, then; take it to heart. Make of it the very beat of the heart. Then the Word comes alive; it speaks to commonality and praxis. Do it. Do the Word.

Thus too, judgment comes home. It is lodged against our own culture, against our contempt for the poor, our wars and injustice and greed.

~

As we read, Jesus stands at our side. He speaks for the victims, the forgotten ones, those who live and die in the margins of the text, in the footnotes, the silence, the space between letters. Be attentive. In the scroll hear the voice of the dead, the unborn, the expendable.

FIRST BOOK OF KINGS

Who Shall Inherit the Grand Years of David?

(Chs. 1–4)

Your house and your kingdom shall be made sure forever before me; your throne shall be established forever.

2 Samuel 7:16

Solomon Enthroned (Ch. 1)

Our scene opens on a charming note: the last years of David. He is enfeebled; a beautiful young woman is introduced to serve the royal needs. (And, as usual, the text is silent in her regard. No reaction is recorded to this unusual tour of duty.)

Meantime, all is not well in the realm. As previously noted, the family of David is adroit in the crafts of power: who shall rise and who fall, who shall win the spoils and who pay up. No wonder, then, around the deathbed of the regent cabals simmer, intrigues threaten outright rebellion.

~

First in secret, then openly, a son of David, Adonijah, adopts the ways of his brother Absalom: he mounts an insurrection and declares himself king. He is joined by a formidable ally, the general of the armies, Joab, nephew of the king.

This Joab is a puzzle. Again and again (as we recall from 2 Samuel)

13

he risked life and limb for David. Then he showed quite another side: a turncoat.

~

Nathan appears on the scene; his presence proves crucial. (He will be remembered for a rare confrontation; David stands guilty of adultery and murder [2 Sam. 12:1-15]).

Nathan is politically adroit. When news of the conspiracy reaches his ears, he immediately consults with Bathsheba, mother of Solomon. Let her speed to the bedside of David and plead the cause of their son. Solomon, no other, must be certified as king. He, Nathan, will immediately second her, reinforcing her plea with his own.

The plot thickens. Small peace upon final days! David must again face the choler and effrontery of his family.

~

A relief. The two virtuous conspirators, Bathsheba and Nathan, prevail. At point of death, David hands the scepter to Solomon. And for the first time, a rite of passage is observed in a series of ceremonies and symbols, all quite grand. A cortege is mounted; the candidate is anointed; trumpets sound. The people acclaim the new king; he is enthroned; homage is rendered by chief officials.

~

Solomon is king. The news is brought in some detail to the pretender Adonijah. With this addition: the officials who paid homage to the new king also visited with the aged David. Answering their felicitations, the dying king prostrated himself in prayer, saying, "Blessed be Yahweh, the God of Israel, who has permitted me to see this day, one of my descendants seated on the throne."

We note that the title "God of Israel" is invoked in the prayer. The accession of Solomon is seen as the continuation of a providential act: long ago Saul was rejected and David, beloved of Yahweh, attained the throne.

Another implication: Solomon enhances legitimacy and continuity.

And the pretender Adonijah is cast into the dark camp of rejection where Saul languished.

~

With the studied, awkward gestures of a morality play, the story proceeds. Panic reigns in the ranks of Adonijah. Former cronies take to their heels. The pretender is left to his fate. He too cuts and runs, to the tent of covenant, its altar and four horns. Seeking "sanctuary," he grasps one of these, a spar in a wild sea.

And Solomon, in the flush of triumph, can afford to be magnanimous. He allows his enemy life and freedom, on the stern condition of no further trouble-making.

"Blood Will Have Blood" (2:1-11)

The hour of David's death approaches. In a solemn homily of farewell, he commends to his son observance of the "laws, commandments, ordinances and instructions, according to what was written in the law of Moses."

It reads like a page from a legal tome — which indeed it is, from Deuteronomy, where such redundancies meet the bemused eye.

~

Around the deathbed, it is as though a cloud seized on the sun of midday. Just short of a sparse last breath, David proceeds to a far different act than prayer. No impetration, no mercy. Only "vengeance is mine."

What a scene! The first and worst offender is none other than David's chief of staff, Joab. His recent collusion with Adonijah goes unmentioned; worse crimes by far haunt the dying king.

Foulest is the murder of Abner, son of Saul's general. A tangled web! David had reconciled with Abner, and the latter pledged his good offices. Further, Joab treacherously murdered Amasa, nephew of David, probably for his collusion with Absalom.

Blood will have blood. Vengeance and holy wars are two sides of a single coin. Through the sword of Joab, for a lifetime David pursued his enemies like an exterminating angel. But against his general he could do no ill. Self-interest stayed the sword; Joab was perpetually useful to royal designs.

Nevertheless. The memory of David is demonically persistent and lucid. No place for forgiveness! Clear the ground. Let Solomon start afresh, choosing his own counselors and generals.

Therefore the dire instruction: Joab must die: "You will act wisely; allow no white hairs of his head to descend into Sheol in peace."

~

Solomon is to be accounted wise above all others? In the eyes of David, the proof of wisdom is worldly, relentless, unforgiving — as vengeance requires, let the sword be unsheathed.

~

There remains a further item: the matter of one Shimei, who, along the road of the king's exile, leveled curses and cast stones and offal. The rub: David has forgiven his tormenter; more, he has bound himself by oath to do him no harm (2 Sam. 19:23-24).

But, but — the bile of memory rises, all but choking the royal throat. How undo the knot of the oath? Casuistry will come on a way.

This way: son Solomon is bound by no such promise. And — a capital matter — the malediction uttered that day against David remains in force. It must at all costs be turned back. Turn it back then, Solomon!

And again, with an irony altogether blind, David appeals to the "wisdom" of his son.

It is like invisible writing. First a text; then, half hidden, a counter. Thus early in the Solomonic reign, our scribe lets fall a hint: the quality of the adduced royal wisdom. In effect, we see a pointing finger, a verbal indirection, enticement to murder lauded as wisdom.

The move is native to a jungle. Remove enemies, settle old scores. Thus, by "whatever means," reign supreme.

~

"You, son Solomon, wise in your ways, will know what to do." The tactic is a kind of mafioso hint. It is as though from the papery lips of a fading godfather, a roundabout instruction were whispered: "You will know. . . ."

And, as events unfold, the hint is accurately taken. Let Joab be prevented from reaching old age. Shimei, on the other hand, is already old; it is "the white hair of his head" which must be sent to hell. Let it burn there.

Young or old — no matter. The matter is vengeance. With a trembling gesture David reaches out: "You, you must avenge wrongs done me!"

∾

Sic transit gloria. As he lived, so David dies. And wittingly or no, the historian is merciless in his mercy, toward us as well, disabled as we are by a like, latter-day culture of death. We stand greatly in need of instruction on matters of enmity, vengeance — and, let it be added, instruction on the despised alternative: forgiveness.

Forgiveness? The word lies weeping in the shadows, like a dying Iraqi child.

∾

Dispassionately, with surgical skill, the testament of a king is recorded. And we make of the scene what we will, what our lives bring to it.

From David, no sign of repentance. No mention, no inkling of such. Quite the contrary: his last breath reeks. Underscored in the text: blood will have blood. The legacy is blood.

∾

Comments, explanations, one thinks, often amount to a form of cultural reduction. At times, footnotes allow custom and culture to shed light on behavior. They also may usefully explain certain lapses — or attempt to.

But we note with a kind of shamed relief: no such comment is offered here. A rare integrity rules the text. We are to take the medium, the bare bones of narrative, for the message. This: David dies intemperate, transfusing his venom into the veins of his son.

∾

Sic transit David rex. His last hours are simply thrust at us; awful, sple-
netic. Comment, whether of excuse or denunciation, is redundant —
even perhaps offensive to a thoughtful eye. Let the episode speak for itself.

What of a title? Here is one: "How Not to Die." Or another: "The Descent of David into Hell — on Earth" (but surely the descent was underway years before).

~

In such wise, we biblical folk of another time are invited to ponder a
far different wisdom than is urged from the royal couch of passing.

Or yet another tack, an implication, a dangerous one. Suppose this:
we choose to pass over the evidence of blood vengeance and curses, dis-
missing such matters as relics of another, more savage age.

A more savage age than ours?

The truth, one thinks, gives pause; it is as large and crude as a public
billboard. It also allows for no illusion, no mistaking the message. In a
different time (our own), blood vengeance and cursing take a form simi-
lar to the tinder which set the bones of David blazing.

A like reality. We know it well, if we know anything: the many-
headed Hydra of our time — war, racism, contempt for the victimized,
duplicitous authority, greed, domination, violent death inflicted, eye-for-
eye vengeance.

And the curse: the incanting of death as "solution," sought after, revered, worshiped; death as a chief cultural principality. Death paid tribute in the research and deployment of weapons of genocide.

~

Ultima Ratio Reagan

The reason we do not learn from history is
Because we are not the people who learned last time.

Because we are not the same people as them
That fed our sons and honor to Vietnam
And dropped the burning money on their trees,

We know that we know better than they knew,
And history will not blame us if once again
The light at the end of the tunnel is the train.

Howard Nemerov

~

David's dying instruction to his son hints, and more, at an accept-able, even laudable behavior and ideology. The imperial status quo is lodged like a speck of radium, ineradicable, in the breast of the king.

The king's son is implicitly commanded to rise and shine, in the image of his father and ancestors, those like-minded warriors and winners.

Be like us — honor the bloodline! is the call. No greater honor to dying David and the new king both than the mimesis intact.

Let matters be put plain. The hand of David grasps the hand of son Solomon. Then the dying father speaks: "Be strong, then, and show yourself a man."

~

A man? Not, be it noted, "show yourself human."

But how, in any case, could Solomon "show himself human"? What example is offered by parent, advisor, peer for the youth to draw on? What icons is he to emulate?

The imperial culture is a sham, a front, sterile, alienated from holiness and true valor. Before the gaze of young Solomon lies the dying king, this chameleon figure of scorn and stealth, of tenderness and ferocity. David's last hour, crowning a tumultuous life. His last hour — and arguably his worst.

~

If young Solomon turns and glances beyond, he views a vast, teeming horizon, the empire. Moral grandeur there, access to the truth of life? Alas, small measure of these, or none at all. His chief authorities (counselors and warriors, courtiers and priests and teachers of the law) form a tight circle of ethical clones.

And beyond, scarcely discernible, stand figures of privilege and power, together with their victims: masters and slaves, keepers and prisoners, soldiers innumerable, money lenders and debtors, the affluent and beggars, winners and losers of every stripe. Those who batten off misery; those who pay up. The Davidic "system" in sum. Shortly to be known across the world as the Solomonic system — one and the same, only bigger, louder, richer: a juggernaut.

In the last years of Solomon, void and darkness will befall. In this era as well, no prophets will leaven the mass.

~

An all but forbidden question (therefore, let it be recorded). Shall the new king turn for instruction to this or that woman, mother, servant, slave, or to a prisoner of conscience, a hostage? Shall he discover in unlikely corners and alleys and prisons of the realm, hidden and humiliated, a truth teller?

~

"Show yourself a man." What a phrase, loaded with implications. A vigorous right arm, grasp on a sword, the warrior ethos in action. An itching crotch as well, a sexual spur. And eyes alive to the main chance. In sum, a winner — condemning, even as he creates, losers.

In such ways, through such behavior, "show yourself a man." And for legacy, father to son, a whispered command: blood will have blood; attend to this.

~

The order of instructions, tripartite, is also of interest. Solomon is to "be strong, show yourself a man" in the first instance by obeying to the tittle the "commands of Yahweh."

Second, by settling scores. Underscore this.

Then let him attend to a far lesser matter, a footnote of sorts — an act of mercy. The last item: reward the sons of Barzillai, who succored David and his men in the desert.

In the king's mind, the instruction is hyphenated. We discover no hint of embarrassment — quite the opposite — in the weird linkage. Obedience to God, then vengeance, and finally, tardily, an act of compassion.

~

Let us leave David to expire in peace. A peace which might seem to the thoughtful eye ambiguous if not unearned.

To his last breath, does the king lack an essential of soul? He dies, steeped in a strange innocence. His crimes stand there, ghosts with lengthening shadows, mute witnesses — crimes devoid of consequence.

Leave David where he lies. Knowing as we do — or do not — better ways of living and dying. Our legacy is Jesus and the saints.

"The Wisdom of Solomon" (2:12-46)

Shadowy Adonijah lurks in the wings, hardly inclined to put aside his machinations. The king is dead; another than the pretender has won the throne. Still, an odor of intrigue lingers. Enveloped in it, Adonijah approaches Bathsheba. Would she deign to intercede, winning a favor from the new king?

The favor seems, on the face of it, a small matter. Adonijah seeks the hand of Abishag of Shunem, the maiden who had warmed the limbs of David in his last days.

~

"The wisdom of Solomon"! The tribute has passed into the conventional lore of the tribe. But in what measure the gift will enhance a given occasion remains unclear.

Early in the long reign of Solomon, Bathsheba approaches the throne. We witness the exchange. And the famed "wisdom" appears less exalted than commonly lauded. It comes to something quite quotidian, one thinks. To this: Solomon's sharp common sense, a sense that flourishes under pressure of ego, truculence, greed, or lust.

Put simply, Solomon is no fool. He is in fact uncommonly canny; his weighing of the worth of others, of the moment to leap, to sidestep, to plant himself, is acute. His eye roves this way and that. What odor does the prevailing wind bear along? An odor, so to speak, of agenda wafting his way?

So to our episode. Bathsheba is unaware of a certain provision of the law. It will surface later, and crucially. (Woman as she is, ignorance cruelly befits. Ignorance is bliss — or hell.)

Moreover, given the demeaning estate of her sisters of the harem, Bathsheba should properly be grateful. In the text she is granted a name.

～

Solomon, as goes without saying, bears a name — one to be reckoned with, a name above all names. And more: a title, a throne. Need it be added that he dwells above such petty matters as may be thought to occupy women?

On occasion, the great one pleases his soul by an act of magnanimity. Let Bathsheba be heard. Hearing, his face grows inflamed. A small matter looms into a large one, nefarious: usurpation! The word sticks in the throat of the king. For thus it is written in the law: whoever takes possession of even one woman of the harem of a defunct king, that one attains right of succession to the throne.

Is this not strange? An extraordinary power rests in a coven of nameless women. To choose, even in the act of being chosen — to choose the one who shall sit on the throne!

But — will they succeed in exercising that power? Did it happen that a woman could say to her soul, to the public, to history, "I have tipped the scales"?

For prosperous functioning of the system, let nothing of the like be allowed. In the imperium, shall a ruler be chosen by women? And in consequence, shall someone favorable toward women mount the throne? Banish the thought! A far different outcome is implied, inevitable, resting in the common understanding, in the (male) text. In the harem system itself.

～

As appears here once again, the acclaimed royal wisdom is in fact a quite pedestrian matter: conventional skills, strongly bent toward survival. Skills like a number of sticks, tied together, forming fasces. And a threat as well: an ax in the center of the bundle.

Is Solomon a proto-fascist? Is not every absolute monarch?

~

Skills, survival. Thus the reasoning of Solomon: "My older brother he is, and he seeks the hand of Abishag. Is he not seeking the throne as well?"

Adonijah seeks it, beyond doubt. Too clever by half, the schemer has sealed his fate. Brother or no brother, he is executed forthwith.

Thence Solomon turns to unfinished matters, a solemn burden, the legacy of David. First the traitorous high priest Abiathar is stripped of his powers and banished.

Then to a more complicated affair: that of general Joab. David, as his son knows, was heavily in debt to this noble subaltern. By every canon Joab is owed gratitude; he protected the life of David and preserved his throne.

Still. Certain crimes of the general were beyond countenancing. David lay dying; the memory rankled.

Solomon reflects: Joab murdered "two men, more just and honorable than himself; and this without the knowledge of my father David."

The two who perished, we recall, were generals of the armies of Israel and Judah.

Joab senses danger closing in. Like Adonijah, he flees to the ark, in hope of sanctuary. But Solomon is undeterred. He knows the law, and it favors him: "When a man kills another after scheming to do so, you must take him even from my altar and put him to death" (Exod. 21:14).

The tension heightens. The executioner approaches; he orders Joab outside. He must not be slain on sacred ground.

Joab will not obey. "No, I shall die here."

Back to the king, with a report of the proceedings. And the instruction is repeated; the decree is ineluctable: "Then slay him where he clings, at the altar!"

So it was done.

~

Next, deal with the notorious Shimei, who cursed David along exile road: "You will know what to do."

Indeed, Solomon the wise will know. But there is an obstacle. Shimei has committed no crime.

Nonetheless. Now and again, crime must be manufactured whole cloth.

Under pain of death an order is issued. Shimei may not depart from Jerusalem. And Solomon bides his time. For three years, Shimei obeys. Then, two slaves flee his house; he pursues and apprehends them. Solomon seizes the long-sought pretext. The fate of the offensive one is sealed.

~

These great ones render their religion in a mixed vat of superstitions, incantations, projections. Thus blessings and curses take on an overbearing vitality and perdurance.

A blessing is like a blank check drawn against consequence. And a curse clings like sex and source, a succubus. The oppositions, curse/blessing, clash with ungovernable force, in good or ill fortune of the one they fall upon.

Thus the superstition: for every curse (here, the curse uttered years before by Shimei), there must be uttered a counter: a blessing.

Fervently the king utters it, incanting good fortune, forfending ill: "Blessed be Solomon, and may the throne of David subsist before Yahweh forever!"

~

Thus certain delicate matters, neglected while David lived, are disposed of. Ever so quietly, dossiers are closed. And in the closure, aspects of the character of Solomon emerge.

As for the deathbed injunction of his father, he is indeed "strong," he "shows himself a man." He is also obedient to the jot and tittle of "the laws, the commands, the ordinances and instructions. . . ."

Dreams and Shadows of Dreams (Ch. 3)

3:3

Is an encomium intended, or reproof and judgment? It could be either; the text leaves it to us. In any case, one matter is clear. Like father, like son: Solomon conducted his affairs in accord with the principles of his father David.

"Principles" — a curious word, perhaps ironic; one hopes so. In context: the behavior of David was that of a nimble trickster, governed by a chameleon ethic. Solomon must also be excused for worshiping in forbidden places (according to the principles of his father David?), with one notorious exception: he sacrificed and burned incense "on the high places."

As for the new king's subjects, are these not generationally favored? Do they not behold in the son a ruler according to the heart of the father?

From the start one is tempted to name Solomon a clone of David.

And a consummate bore as well.

3:4-15

There remains the bestowal of divine blessing on the new king. The sooner the better, then — let it rain down, a danaian shower of gold.

One night, Solomon is granted a notable dream.

And why not? The age of the prophets lies far in the future. So Yahweh seeks a nocturnal entrance, as has occurred from time immemorial.

We recall a strong biblical tradition of dreams of substance, of dreams that change everything — for the dreamer, for the people. We have Jacob's dream at Bethel, together with its extravagant promise (Gen. 28:10-19). Then a second dream: dreamer Jacob is urged to return to the land of his birth (Gen. 31:10-13). And we have the dream of Abimilech, with its daunting threat (Gen. 20:3-7).

~

And once more a crucial dream, signifying a breakthrough of note. Solomon, man of action, repairs to the shrine of Gibeon; he would offer sacrifice there. He falls to rest, and the nocturnal visitation opens, a momentous, vividly peopled diorama. Yahweh, it seems, is appeased, and more, vastly pleased by the fealty of his regent.

As to the message, we wonder, Who conveyed it to our storyteller? If its source is Solomon himself, the more reason to stress its highly subjective, self-fulfilling character.

The scene is charged with projection. We conjure the youthful regent, flushed with power and glory, actual and anticipated. And lo! Yahweh appears, likewise flushed with the power and glory of Solomon. For the asking, gifts — any gifts imaginable — flow from the divine cornucopia tipped.

Seek, then, and you shall find. And in dream as in waking, Solomon is — shall we say — canny? He implores a gift already (in the sense suggested above) his: wisdom. With practiced skill, the dreamer bows and scrapes a bit. Surely he can afford to: "I am a young man, and know little or nothing about ruling."

Then, warming to the tactic, he magnifies the difficulties faced by this callow ruler — himself: ". . . amid a people you have chosen, so numerous no one could number them."

Then he makes the request: "Grant your servant a heart apt to judge good and evil, fit to govern your great people."

On the moment, according to our chronicler, the gift is granted.

But, but. As to the working out of this finely tuned discernment, outpoured here in mellifluous measure, we shall see.

~

And what of this god of Solomon, the giver of all good things? Are we to conclude that the king's dream has brought to his side the Holy One, the Yahweh of Abraham, Isaac, and Jacob? We are perhaps entitled to reservations, even to doubts.

To name a few of these:

– The memory of David is invoked, his example commended to the son. According to the god, the father is an icon unblemished: "If you obey my commands, as your father did. . . ."

– David obeyed? One must scrutinize closely the nature of the commands. "Obey" the anathema? We conclude that two agents, god and regent, colluded in crime. That being so, the praise is comprehensible, the command abhorrent.

– One notes that (1) the memory of Yahweh is highly selective, and that (2) notions held by the divinity as to an ethical code strangely resemble those of the king himself. Nimbus and warts, both intact.

— The quality of gifts conferred seems rhetorically extravagant: "I give you a heart wise and intelligent, the likes of which has not been, nor shall be."

— Material gifts are promised in abundance, a reward for not having sought them. But these are laced with moral ambiguity; they are dangerous gifts: "riches and glory, the equal of which has never been seen among kings."

Solomon (and presumably his patron) will rue the day. And the dream.

~

Whatever the substance of the nocturnal event, the realm of Solomon is off to a heady start. The new king is sure of mind; the god has declared himself, irrevocably. And even in dream, how well Solomon has acquitted himself: how modest his words, how wise his request for wisdom!

The scene glows with golden promise, a veritable Tintoretto canvas.

Yet here and there, in a faultless world taking shape, shadows gather.

~

"If you follow my ways, keep my laws and my commands . . . I will grant you a long life."

The direction of those "ways," the substance of the "laws" — such details as these, troublesome and crucial, are yet to be revealed. And when they are, much will be found wanting in the performance of his majesty.

~

In Israel and elsewhere, the episode that follows will become a touchstone of the king's wisdom. The gift, its fame, will reach afar. The story also forges a link with other oriental literature, in which the rendering of just judgment is lauded as a chief virtue.

~

Toward the end of the era of Kings, Isaiah will venture a caveat. He insists that in principle the nations (including, by implication, the realm of Solomon, assimilated to the structures and ethos of the surrounding kingdoms) — these "nations" remain ignorant of the demands of justice. More: they lack the spiritual capacity to enact the demands. Works of justice, the prophet implies, are hardly native to imperialists. Such virtuous action follows on an impulse of grace, a gift of God, conveyed to whom God will.

And the choice of recipient is laced with irony and sorrow. According to the prophet, the practice of justice is wrought by no king. Rather, the transcendent skill belongs to a servant of Yahweh — a suffering servant, to be sure. By one who, in awful contrariety, must bear the brunt of imperial injustice. A difficult vocation, a veritable martyrdom. The servant speaks on behalf of the victims. And for that pays heavily:

"... until (s)he establish justice on the earth."
And again, more directly:
"I, Yahweh, have called you for the victory of justice." (Isa. 42:4, 6)

A caveat indeed, if not a contradiction to the claims of Solomon, conventional and self-serving.

3:16-28

To our Solomonic episode. We have here a high point of his realm, the wisdom of the young king at apogee.

Entering the royal presence are two prostitutes. Each bears at breast an infant. On a close look, it is evident that one is living, the other a corpse. Each of the women heatedly claims the living child for her own, ranting that the rival has substituted a corpse in place of the living.

What is the king to do? He calls for a sword, and makes as though to divide the surviving child in two, half for each claimant. One woman agrees to the Draconian solution. But the other cries in anguish, relinquishing her claim. "Do not kill the child. Give it to her!" And the king's voice rings out, cutting the Gordian knot: "This one is the mother. Give her the child!"

An admirable sagacity.

The king, we note, is unspoilt by imperial ego, undistracted by vast projects to come, those monuments of glory — the palace, the temple, and the encircling wall of Jerusalem.

A rare and refreshing moment. Solomon bends to the conflicted sorrow of two women, cultural dregs, lacking even the shadowy favor of the king's harem. Yet they are granted ready access and a humane outcome. The story is vivid and heartfelt in the telling.

The Apotheosis of Empire (Ch. 4)

To backtrack briefly: The king has moved quickly, audaciously, to take an Egyptian wife (3:1). His decision underscores the resorgimento of Israel, as well as the steep decline in the fortunes of Egypt. (Centuries earlier, we are told, a pharaoh would regard a foreign alliance as plain impertinence. How far we have come! our writer suggests.)

Now Solomon proceeds to set up an impressive bureaucracy of "high officials." Naming them in detail, the historian conveys the aura of a self-confident ruler, determined to set his imprint on the times and the future. To stand as an equal, if not to surpass his imperial neighbors.

Evidently temple and palace are considered a twin entity. Along with other functionaries, a chief priest is named. Religious activities are thus defined by implication and controlled in fact.

It perhaps goes without saying: Solomonic religion will grant no place to dissenters or critics, should such unlikelies show face. No such incursions are recorded. The robe of empire is seamless and immaculate. No second thoughts intrude, no critique.

We stand at a threshold, a dawn: the apotheosis of empire approaches. And might it be that the two phenomena are linked: the prospering of empire and the absence of prophets?

~

We are to know it, in some detail: they live well, this potentate and his courtiers, generals, priests, intermediaries, secretaries, prefects, camp followers. "They ate and drank and made merry."

Good for them. For tomorrow . . . ?

~

And that wisdom again — we never are done with hearing of it. In a strange, rather mixed metaphor, our writer says, "God gave him an extraordinarily great intelligence, and a heart vast as the sands of the sea shore."

The myth is in full play; the day is at apogee; the Solomonic renown knows no horizon. Only imagine the omnigatherum, the total sway of imperial mind! The king's mind is equable and populous; he composes a thousand proverbs and an equal number of songs; he discourses knowingly of "plants, beasts, birds, reptiles and fishes."

And from parts known and unknown, delegations arrive in Jerusalem, hungering for the savor of his wisdom.

What, we ask, somewhere between dazzlement and disbelief, what is transpiring here? An extended reign is lodged in the memory of scribes and priests and people, an era of unalloyed, even magical achievement, from about 960 to 920 C.E.

~

National consciousness is taking form — imperial form, to be sure. A people seizes the reins of history, magnifying its ancestral story. Tribal traditions meld in themes of achievement and supremacy.

In the glories wrought by Solomon, splendidly dilated, the lure of David's line comes to fruition, a scepter to hand, a crown to brow. All hail, this social, political, military, aesthetic, architectural, religious, even technological achievement!

~

A people hold a golden mirror aloft. They see Solomon; they see themselves — a nation favored on high, citizens of the kingdom united (for a time). Thus, through the monarch, glory accrues (for a time).

Let us dare be critical. Any pagan realm, to ensure its glory, would thus record it: Babylon, Egypt, and later, Rome. A text like this one.

But in the broad scope of the story of Israel — call it intrusion, correction, excoriation — the prophets and their God will be heard from, amending the "official" text before our eyes. This "second text," this "correction from below," is unheard of in other royal records.

Talk about midrash!

~

For a time (for a time only), Solomon can do no ill, brook no rival, no critique or challenge — only heyday and honeymoon. Thus reports his chronicler, and the people echo the theme — according to the chronicler.

One senses a strange innocence in the air. It is as though peerless days and years were seen through the wide eyes of a child.

Or another image: as though the ship of state were riding a high crest; as though height and crest were the sole form of the wave of history. As though no menacing trough lurked, a gorge of Leviathan.

Or again, as though genius and good fortune were the sole notes of the symphony we name history. No muttering drumbeat, nothing of tragedy, no shortfall, no ambition thwarted.

Or this: as though in full bloom, the imperial flower bore no seeds of decay. The bloom could never wither, great Solomon never fall from glory.

Fiction, and more: contra naturam. But O how sweet the moment!

Stone upon Stone, the King Constructs Immortality

(Chs. 5–9)

In every government, there grows up a hideous Establishment of stupid men.

Graham Greene, *Reflections*

Governments are the knotting together of the worst human instincts.

Anonymous

The "Great Pyramid" of Solomon (Ch. 5)

Remarkable, how well these ancient autarchs, Solomon and his imperial friends, got on together. (Except of course, when they got on badly indeed!)

The times were fortunate — for some. Our tale is sunny — for a while. It summons an era of imperial smiles and outstretched hands, of open borders, mutual stroking, admiration, and advantage. And the clink of gold is reassuring, an era of merchandising gone mad.

World trade brings a smile to the otherwise beetling face of Mars. And a paunch to his warrior frame.

~

The appetitive dreams of imperial ego! A vast project takes shape: King Solomon's Great Pyramid, so to speak.

32

As the pharaoh and other despots are aware, there are three ways of gaining admission to the sun boat and its voyage to immortality: wars won, territory expanded, and grand edifices erected. Happily, Solomon need not launch either the first or second project, father David having "cleansed" the kingdom and secured its borders.

On then to the third! The great king might have composed the saying, "Si monumentum requiris, circumspice." "If you seek his monument, look about you." Or, better still, the motto of Things to Come: "Pay little attention to small matters, large attention to great."

~

Instances accumulate; there exists, alas, a dark side of flowering greatness. Among matters requiring only passing attention, these might be mentioned: taxes and forced labor, class divisions, gang-pressing youths into standing armies, the misery of many and the prospering of few.

To the great ones, small matters. Inevitable, alas, is a degree of "collateral loss" if the works and pomps of the Sun King are to prosper.

~

Another matter comes to mind; it lingers like the scent of a lost garden, lodged gently in memory. Far back in royal recall — if remembered at all — stand two harlots and their infants, the dead child and the living, the young king attentive to the outcasts and their lorn innocent.

~

On to matters of large, even surpassing interest. Hiram, the king of Tyre, felicitates the new king of Israel. The courtesy invites a response. Solomon seizes on the occasion, welcoming the skills of Tyrian craftsmen on behalf of a Great Project: the construction of a temple in Jerusalem.

The project becomes a near obsession of the king. And given his manic energy and imperial connections, the dream shortly takes solid form.

The hallmark of the dream is the piety of the king, a devotion unmatched — and altogether impure. He will raise high an ambiguous sign, a fitting habitation, image of the god of his heart — an ambiguous god, the patron and fabulist of empire.

~

Solomon sets about negotiating with his pagan neighbors. The message to the king of Tyre is remarkable on several counts. It begins with a revisionist history of David's wars: these unpleasantries, it appears, were thrust upon a peaceable soul, much against his will. Just wars they were, every one.

Solomon then admits to a stalemate on his father's part: he had longed to undertake the vast sanctified construction. Alas, an impediment befell: "wars which his enemies waged against him from all sides." A remarkable whitewash of Davidic buccaneering.

~

Add to the above a repeated invocation of Yahweh. Divine approval of the temple project is steeped in a marinade of rhetoric. The tone is correctly ecumenical as well. By implication, neighbor Hiram will understand the worth of the project. Perhaps because he too is a believer?

Hiram receives the note; on the moment he grows religiously ecstatic: "Blessed be the LORD this day, who . . ."

And one thinks, This god is easily parceled abroad by his imperial devotees. Wonderful! All over the map, this deity is useful.

Thus, from the start, the ideology of Solomon's religion bears a spurious ecumenical tinge: serving the imperial chosen, this god is also advantageous to goys — even as they are to him.

~

Memories too can be made to serve. Do some memories miss the mark of truth? What matter? In retrospect the wars of the Kings are laved in a perfume of virtuous necessity. The motto of the great ones might well be "Winner Take All — Even the Memories."

~

But only wait, we shall have more of this shuffling about of supersensible "reality," a species of "theology from the summit." The god of armies, avers the king, was hardly a neutral in the holy wars: ". . . until such time as Yahweh put those enemies under the soles of his feet."

34

Now, at long last, wars won, borders secured, Solomon proclaims, "Yahweh my god has given me peace on all sides."

The dead are buried out of sight and mind. Now the vast architectural dream can bestow on the god a habitation and a name above all names.

~

First thing first; now to the second. (The sequence, need it be stated, is dictated by status, honor, ego.) Let the lord of earth invoke (indirectly, but surely overheard on high) the lord of heaven: "I purpose the construction of a temple to the name of Yahweh my god, in accord with . . ." — the reference being to the prophecy of Nathan spoken to David. Beyond doubt the foundations will stand steady, mortised with the bones of the fallen.

~

Puzzling, the god-drenched language of Solomon's missive, flowing like oil down the beard of Aaron. And of course the emperor Hiram will cooperate. The trade pact is concluded: lumber in exchange for food supplies.

~

No more ado; now to the labor. Firs and cedars fall. The axes flash in the hands of Phoenicians, endowed with the know-how of foresters and shipbuilders and sea merchants. We all but hear the earth groaning in its innermost parts, as the great trees of Lebanon fall to Solomon's will.

We are impressed — and meant to be, and hardly the first so affected. We marvel at the sheer scope of the undertaking, the multitudes of workers drafted. The scale is daunting. Thousands of this, thousands of that: carriers, stone cutters, artists, sculptors, overseers.

Impressed, we are also ill at ease. A godly project, we are assured. Yet, yet, does it go forward by dint of forced labor? It is as though a crack appeared in the foundations and, despite all remedy, spread.

And what of the temple that rises, its walls of "hewn stone," in contravention of an ancient edict? Was it not commanded that stele or altar stone be left undressed by human hands, in tribute to the transcendent creator of all?

And here is the god, blessing, countenancing every move. How earthbound, one cannot but think, is the celestial project!

The House of the Lord? (Ch. 6)

6:1-10

The winner owns the history, and bends it to his will. No ordinary prelude befits so extraordinary an undertaking. So a solemn organ note is struck, and a daring parallel drawn.

The witnesses — whether these be ancient Israelites or ourselves scanning the text — are seized by an awe that drowns logic. The presumption, the parallel, the daring fiction — all are breathtaking.

What greater glory than this, a dwelling fit for the god of exodus — and of empire?

~

An even more momentous decision awaits. It comes to this. Time itself is drawn into service of the imperial will. Let calendars be altered, if need be.

Thus: we stand in the 480th year since the return from exile and the reconstruction of the nation. And that same year, ground is broken for the construction of the temple. Thus one momentous event summons a second. And who could fail to note the parallel? The later event bears an import equal to the first. Each is providential, each blessed and overseen by Yahweh.

~

And this is implied as well: does not each occurrence require a leader, a visionary who summons the genius of the nation to momentous tasks, Exodus and Temple, one who, with a near omnipotent gesture, brings great events into being — architect of the nation, architect of the temple? Does not each require a very portent, a genius — a Moses in the first instance, a Solomon in the second? Indeed, a Moses-like Solomon?

~

Amid the construction, an oracle; it recalls the promise made to David by Nathan. A voice is heard, and a message. Let all hearken!

It is as though "ruah," the breath of Yahweh, blew like a great wind over the blocks of hewn stone, shook the timbers overhead and gave them speech. For every yin a yang, for every room and wall and ceiling and tapestry and overlay of bronze and gold leaf and munificent furnishing — an inner meaning, a soul and summons.

Now and again, Yahweh sees aright, and speaks up. Here he sounds a note worthy of a Jeremiah or an Ezekiel.

6:11-13

It is as though the stones cried out, protesting, warning. In the melding of genius, sweat, and tears that serves to raise the temple, Solomon and his people must not lose the entelechy, the inner meaning of the great project.

The message from on high: of first import is soul, not stone; is presence, mindfulness, fidelity: "As to the temple you are constructing — "

Yahweh ruminates; the sentence breaks off. But not for long. The theme builds and builds.

The great prophets will never tire of sounding it. A brusque command of Jeremiah: "Put not your trust in deceitful words" (Jer. 7:4). And his mocking incantation: "The temple of the LORD, the temple of the LORD!"

And the warning culminates in the scalding indictment drawn up by the God of Ezekiel. In that era, Yahweh can no longer contain himself — or be contained! The temple has become an anti-temple, a cauldron of idolatry.

The vessel tips and spills over, polluting the common life. From its depths flows a sewer of degradation, a befouled stream of injustice, greed, lust. Such "religion" is lethal to all it touches (Ezek. 8:3-18).

A house of worship, sumptuous, numinous? To this the temple of Solomon will come a sty of swinish souls, a theater in which unbelievers, all ablaze, mime their loss of the true way.

For his part, Yahweh will have none of it. Ezekiel be his witness! In the gesture of an insulted potentate, the God of Glory rises from his throne and departs the temple precincts (Ezek. 8:1-2).

In the lifetime of the prophet, priests and people were long gone in idolatry. The insult stank in the nostrils of the Holy One, beyond bearing. Yahweh must go into exile, dramatizing the fate of God in such a world. A God who abandons those who long since have abandoned God (Ezek. 10:18-19).

~

And this was not the end, but the beginning. There would be other exiles, a multitude driven forth from Jerusalem. Indeed, as Christians too came to understand, Egypt and Babylon became a paradigm, painful but endlessly helpful for a people of faith. Behold us (ourselves behold us), unconformed as we are called to be (and as the apostle urges) to this world (Rom. 12:2). Exiles all.

~

Our text implies a far different time than that decried by Ezekiel. According to the official account, all is sweetness and promise. In the brief span of seven years, the great temple is completed. It stands serene, majestic — a sumptuous domicile for its imperial guest. Everything is excessive; eye and mind are bedazzled.

With the advantage of hindsight, knowing the awful outcome of the grand start, we sense the secret intent of the scribe. Does he imply ever so subtly that ambition and pride have overvaulted, that the great pile reeks of inflation, ego — inevitable decay? Does the inauguration of priestly worship bespeak a secret enticement to idolatry, a mordant underground stream of money and power undermining the great pilings?

From the start, the project lies under a mysterious shadow. How could it not, raised as it is in a spirit of overweening pride?

It is as though a mocking children's chant were heard, issuing from God knows where: ". . . and it all falls down. . . ."

~

The great squared blocks are raised, then lowered in place. And we ponder. On a day named by the God of Isaiah "My day," the dressed stones will be prized from place, tumbled and reduced to rubble. Foreign troops will strip the gold and silver and bronze and precious woods, will gather the rich vessels and cart them off for booty — to the blasphemous banquet of a pagan king.

Alas and alas, we know too much.

A Palace Fit for a King? (Ch. 7)

Of the foregoing, Solomon knows nothing. And if he knew, would he not deride the possibility of such an outcome? Is his rule not supreme, equally in command of outcomes as of beginnings?

On, then, to the next grandiose undertaking. The deity fitly honored, occasion is at hand to honor the royal line (i.e., himself) — in short, by erecting a palace. A much more complex venture than the temple, it will consume thirteen years.

~

It is as though history paused to draw breath. Long gone are the years of shame and humiliation in Egypt, this all but nameless tribe of nomads, forty years in the wilderness, survival chancy, subject to the moods of the deity, turning and turning about, from providential mercy to slaughterous fury.

Gone, too, the tent of the wandering God, the Cloud and Pillar of Fire. And gone, long gone is the (rare!) tribal response: trust in Yahweh for the manna, the waters struck from rock.

No more of these. Now the assurance, the accumulation, the era of great Solomon. The century bears, like a newly minted coin, the profile of a Sun King. The weather is a rain of gold, a glory.

Let the imagination soar, the earth yield its riches. In gold and silver and teak and bronze and marble, foreign and domestic laborers set to work, side by side. Years pass, love's labors not for a moment lost. Temple and palace, excessive, lavish — the gleaming piles befit imperial god and emperor alike.

The Temple Dedicated: Folly, Fiction, Obsession (Ch. 8)

8:1-21

The great tasks are finished: the twin dwellings stand proud under heaven. Together with their deity, the chosen have arrived, in more senses than one. Let them rejoice and be glad, as god and king are installed.

There arrives the day of solemnity, the transfer of the ark of the covenant to the "holy of holies" of the new temple, "under the wings of the cherubim."

~

And lo, amid the fanfare, a mystery. The shekinah, the cloud of unknowing, long vanished in the desert heavens, appears once more, filling the temple with glory. Solomon, a somewhat prosaic being, composes on the spot a brief poem:

Yahweh
is pleased

to dwell
in a cloud,

a cloud
that rests

in a temple
raised

by myself,

for
you,

forever.

~

Solomon's strong point is hardly indirection or metaphor. Here, no missing the point, one thinks. The verse, brief and unremarkable as it is, mingles tribute to the god with stroking of the royal ego, satisfaction, a task well done. Double the claim, then: your dwelling — mine too.

One notes also the imperial assurance; the temple, "raised by myself," will endure "forever." Thus the imperial will arrogates time to itself: no less than the start (and stop), in their course, of the exact stars.

Pure nonsensical arrogance. As though a scepter were waved in the air (or the wand of Moses the wonder worker) and lo! time were made absolute. Something like, "Time we command; take the guise of eternity. Our time shall be all time."

~

Or another implication: the imperial system is the sole admissible system. It yields to no challenge or interruption, no latter-day Moses calling for insurrection, no second exodus of the oppressed. No enemy battering at the gates. And, as goes without saying, no interfering voices pointing to lamentable lacunae in the schema of empire: the victims, the expendables.

"The temple will last forever." The king's structure(s) — whether sacred or secular, military or economic — imply no falling away. The empire is the final form of the body politic, the epitome, the ultimate. My people, rejoice. You have arrived.

(And no prophet to translate in derision: "Poor Solomon, poor people, you have, alas, 'arrived' — at a dead end. Allow me to identify your kind and yourselves: he is a vast slaveholder; you are a species of domestic drudges.")

~

Royal ego is rampant. The king can envision no mortal authority superior to him. Time and history stop with him; he is the looming benevolent (?) emblem of God's parousia.

Must not this be termed idolatrous, as Solomon seizes on the end time, and claims it, as though he had set the clocks of the universe — he and not Yahweh?

In any case, the king is making a capital political point. His prayer is like a raised fist, cunningly gloved in velvet. Over against the king's system no alternatives can be imagined, let alone contrived. Let alone permitted.

~

It is all folly, fiction, obsession. One day, a day snatched from the king's grasp, the "day of Yahweh," the truth will be revealed in blistering ruin, panic, and calamity. A ferocious enemy will reduce Jerusalem to a shambles and herd the high and mighty into exile. Royalty dared play God. But God is not mocked.

~

Meantime, the great occasion is at hand. And we await words of royal wisdom. After all (after Yahweh?), this is Solomon's day.

Alas, his discourse to the people, and the prayer that follows, offer no evidence of genius. They are contrived, rather parched, rather smug, charades of imperial religion on display. A supposition is dwelt on, wearyingly: the god stands with the king; in the holy of holies an imperial deity holds court — and hearkens.

Such a day as this, such a king, such a god on high! On earth as in heaven, transcendence and access are in baroque flower. The king looks beseechingly to heaven; the skies rain beneficence. The consonance is like a Jesuit trompe-l'oeil ceiling by Bernini.

~

An imperial god in heaven; and on earth — Solomon. By every supposition and evidence, this is implied, baroquely. The god approves the imperium, its wars and plunders, its forced laborers (a multitude of whom, as we recall, were drafted for construction of the temple), the social class schema, the rich and the impoverished.

Such a system, we note, is new on the biblical scene; among the faithful it had not existed in the "days of unlikeness to the nations," when the contrivances of pagans and their gods (including their arrogant towers) were forbidden.

And now? All, all is changed. Economic, military, and diplomatic structures of "the nations" stand free in temple and palace, and claim the heart of the king. Solomon converses and connives with royal cronies, the rulers of earth. They are equals all; they hold what one would name today "a like worldview." They amass riches (today, read "oil"); wars, diplomacy, and world markets name their game; prosperity, pontification, emissaries, and merchants wend in and out of open borders, sail afar in quest of markets.

And in Jerusalem, a huge bureaucratic apparatus — political, military, economic, religious — is in place. The day of "likeness unto the nations" is at its zenith.

~

In the social fabric of empire, there is a further point of common understanding. It is subtle, and seldom dwelt on. The day of Solomon is also, and inevitably, the day of the god who is "likened to the gods of the nations." In possession of heaven and earth are the favoring one and his (sic) favorite. Each is a potentate, an absolute monarch.

It is as though each held a golden mirror before the other, found the image of the other fair, pleasing, striking in resemblance.

~

And need it be added? As far as can be known, no prophetic troublemakers show face, marring the mirror, beclouding the perfection of event. (Or worse, seize the mirror, flinging it to earth.)

No unseemly voices interrupt the rites. No cries on behalf of the enslaved, the domestic colons, the undocumented, the "widow and orphan."

One marvels. Why were there no prophets? Is the absence a rebuke? Or did one or another arise, to be dealt with summarily, their words, even their names removed from the text?

Grateful, one day we shall welcome great spirits to our bible, our hearts. In dark times we will know and invoke them.

~

But for the time of Solomon, prophetic absence becomes an ominous form of judgment, the Solomonic heyday a form of darkness. Great

Solomon cannot so much as imagine the darkness in which he wanders, all but bereft of scrutiny and judgment.

What need of such? Thus he might inquire in a terrifying innocence. Is not his universe self-contained, his wisdom plenary?

Yet he lies under a curse: no prophets. Or perhaps: prophets forbidden. Or this (as in our day too), prophets put to silence.

~

A Task
In fear and trembling, I think I would fulfill my life
Only if I brought myself to make a public confession
Revealing a sham, my own and of my epoch:
We were permitted to shriek in the tongue of dwarfs and demons
But pure and generous words were forbidden
Under so stiff a penalty that whoever dared to pronounce one
Considered himself as a lost man.

Czeslaw Milosz

~

The grandezza of the Day of Dedication; the occasion sweeps aside earthbound realities and voices. On such a day, the poor and victimized, the beggars, the homeless, the "widows and orphans" dear to the prophets — those social embarrassments simply do not exist. Implied in the splendid, solemn text: Such are swept from the splendid, solemn text. For the nonce they are "disappeared." An old tactic — and a new.

Let no one, nothing, mar the day of days. The gala atmosphere, the strains of self-congratulation, the perfect congruence of heaven and earth! And we are invited to ponder: silly, self-deluded Solomon. His religion would hardly pass muster with a Hosea or an Isaiah. A frosty, scornful eye would deride the spectacle.

~

The scene suggests this: we have on the king's part a detached sense of a god of detachment.

High noon, no shadows. Human and divine ordinances are synchro-

44

nized. Let nothing, no human need or lack, no injustice or suffering impede this lofty intercourse.

~

As for the king's homily, we may be pardoned for confessing an onset of boredom. Five times the name of Yahweh is invoked. "The name" dwells in the new temple; but the temple cannot exhaust or localize the god's immensity. So goes the theology, and to a degree the king's understanding.

In question here is not orthodoxy as such — which is to say, right thinking, right naming of God. That formal "rightness" may to a degree be intact; it may also be sterile of works, the royal praxis a moral void.

The royal behavior a void? The possibility is inadmissible. So good, so felicitous is the throne, it merits the ultimate credential: the god decrees that it thrive.

Prior to "the Day," our text has implied it. The sovereign will is in command of heaven and earth; the empire is, quite simply, the temporal, political form of heaven on earth. We have here, one thinks, a blasphemy masked as a blessing.

~

On to the king's homily, a fairly conventional sampling of imperial rhetoric. (Indeed, throughout history the likes of Solomon are notorious for issuing a summons to one god or another.)

The deity is both stroked and instructed; signs and wonders are urged. And let the deity continue, please, to bestow his (sic) favor.

Thus bespoken, the royal sentiments offer useful, though perhaps unwitting, instruction. This: the god so addressed (and presumably nodding approval from on high) — this one can hardly be considered true God. Whatever the name and claim, Solomon is invoking a baal.

~

An interjection. The foregoing critique is offered as a challenge to a number of commentators. Many among them present the homily of Solomon in a far different light — as virtuous, truthful, an admirable pattern of prayer. Alas, another reading is plausible. The royal homily and prayer are drenched in royal ego. Grand suppositions bedazzle the eye — suppositions hard to support or verify. Like these:

- In the temple deity, king, and people have access to true God.
- The God of truth (the God of Isaiah and Jeremiah) would approve the royal behavior as described above.
- The covenant can be summed up in this manner: a call to the people to consent to, submit to, or at the least be silent before shady if not wicked patterns of rule.

~

To sum up the message of "the Day" (making hay, meantime, of its omissions):

- Let women be silent. Worse, let them be ill-used or shunted aside, as required.
- Let the poor remain unsuccored; destitution is their destiny.
- Let taxes lie heavy, the same monies that support royal excess.
- Let the armed forces proclaim to enemies real or imagined, foreign or domestic, that ours is an insuperable god of battles. Would any presume to take advantage of us? They are hereby warned.

~

In the homily too, one is struck by the manipulation of memory. The son quotes David. Solomon recalls, at third hand, words of his father.

King David, insists the son, was addressed by Yahweh "directly," in this wise: "Since the day I brought my people Israel out of Egypt . . ."

So much for that. Then a shift of attention; the voice of Solomon is raised on his own behalf: "I have constructed a house for the name of Yahweh."

We have noted the audacity. Raising the imperial temple is presented as the apogee; this is the supreme intervention of Yahweh on behalf of the ancestors. From slavery, only imagine, the chosen have come to this Day, this Temple.

One thinks — a lyric leap indeed, across the grandest of canyons.

∽

In our text the Deuteronomists are having their say — and then some. According to them, the god has approved the line of David from the start. Now the same deity has agreed to a change of venue: he will deign to dwell in the king's temple. Thus goes the theme of the king's homily, overlong as it is — indeed, sesquipedalian. And the equally wearying prayer.

8:22-54

The god, magnified mightily, is now directly invoked and the memory of father David summoned. With a petition in mind: let the god be pleased to honor the promise made to father David, to wit: the kingly line will remain intact in perpetuum.

Solomon thus scores a capital point. To empires, whether Babylonian, Egyptian, Assyrian, Israelite, or later, Greek or Roman, one or another deity grants an indispensable gift. The royal line must proceed "forever" — a rather pretentious, improbable confabulation. Altogether likely, one thinks, it will evaporate in a wobbly world.

∽

Nonetheless, Solomon's prayer merits close attention. It hints at the governing ideology of rulers of every time and clime. We have seen it implied before. The likes of Solomon cannot fairly imagine — let alone permit — an alternative or competing political arrangement. Including, let us venture, a revival of the ancient theocracy, or the institution of Judges.

Or, dare one mention the unspeakable? Is this to be tolerated: the appearance of liberators or prophetic opponents of "things as they are"? A Moses, an Isaiah? Heaven forfend. The best is here; the highest is now; the present is the measure of all. Why then palaver about a hypothetical, even illusionary rival arrangement, let alone a "better"?

The empire must stand firm; this is the law. And such security is best ensured under divine approval. Thus Solomon's understanding.

∽

His realm is taking the somber, threatening guise of a "security state." An apparatus of military might, money, conspicuous consumption, and terror is in place. Overweening architecture arises; official pieties hum in the winds. And all is geared to one end: present prospering (for a few) and the perdurance of the social organization (likewise in favor of a few).

In this closed orbit, in the closure of the mind of Solomon, alternatives wither — or, daring to show face, would be crushed.

∿

What I call middle-class society is any society that becomes rigidified in pre-determined forms forbidding all evolution, all gains, all progress, all discovery. I call middle class a closed society in which life has no taste, in which the air is tainted, in which ideas and men [sic] are corrupt. And I think that a man who takes a stand against this death is in a sense a revolutionary.

Frantz Fanon, *Black Skin, White Masks*

∿

But back to the Great Day. In his prayer, Solomon reveals more than he reckons. What does the king most desire; and conversely, what merits small time or attention? Near the start of the prayer, and in a strange time warp, sinfulness is acknowledged, and pardon sought. (Of interest: references to sin and consequence, especially vv. 33-34 and vv. 46-53, are additions to the text, dating from the exile four centuries later.)

Pieties and blindness. The people, returning from exile, are to ". . . entreat you in this temple."

∿

How know the terrifying outcome of pieties and blindness? It is as though the king were evoking the World Trade Center in New York, that Topless Tower of Money. In a terrible hour it fell to rubble.

On an equally terrible day, Solomon's temple and palace will fall to rubble.

∿

48

And a further question. To the king's mind, what constitutes sin? Inevitably, its naming (better, its misnaming) is heavily influenced by the culture of empire. And the chief author and bearer of the culture himself has, alas, small understanding of the sins endemic to his kind. Sins of injustice, sins of sanctioned murder.

How could he confess, renounce, repair? Whence his moral code? He breathes the air, fetid or bracing, of the institutions he brought into being or enlarged in scope and control — good, indifferent, wicked as these may be.

Small matter: good, indifferent, wicked. The god dwells in the temple; all's well with the world. And no voice is raised to decry or fulminate or invoke a better God.

~

For all the apparatus of glory, Solomon is a king unclothed. We note the petrified apparatus of orthodoxy: the subservient priesthood, clients beholden (and secretly envious), the conscience of prince and people befogged. Premise and practice inhibit moral clarity. In sum, the Solomonic culture is puffed by near nonentities, intent on domination and prospering, cost what these may — to others.

Where is the prophetic "voice at the edge"? Who will unmask the king's defaults, denounce the delusional grandeur, the contempt for the poor, the greed and violence, the injustice and moral callousness?

Solomon's prayer falls back on generalities, abstractions: "When they will have sinned against you . . ."

"They." The third person shoves reality off the page. Sinners, one notes, are elsewhere, elsewhen, elsewho, unidentified "others." The high and mighty, for their part, are sinless.

~

We take heart nonetheless. One day truth tellers will reclaim the Decalogue, will confront in a wild fire the crimes of the great ones. The prophets will discomfit, denounce, insist on alternative behavior and structures — and, best of all, will exemplify a godly ethic.

And for the people's sake, long resigned as they are to the royal

dogma, "extra imperium nulla salus" ("outside the empire, no salvation")
— for their sake the prophets will deride these altitudinous follies.

~

We have not yet reached the end of a verbose day.

Still, the long addition to the king's prayer (vv. 41-51) offers a rather wonderful breakthrough.

A breakthrough, but hardly due to Solomon, who must be thought incapable of such. We have a postscript dating from the exile in Babylon, that time of bitter wounds and unlikely healing.

Our midrash merits close, prayerful attention. First, a petition is offered on behalf of strangers at the gate. "Strangers," it is implied, is a darkly encoded word, best dealt with gingerly. Those who stand at the door are hardly "strange" to those within, presupposing a believing people and a summons to hospitality. In truth, those who seek relief, together with those they approach for help, are not strangers at all. They are kinsfolk, sisters and brothers. And this remains true, though the needy arrive late on the scene (and late as well in the scriptures).

The blessed fact that the "strangers" are mentioned at all is hardly due to a sudden grace granted Solomon. It is due to something else, something far deeper.

~

One must undergo it to know it. Precious is the experience that brings new knowledge in its wake — though the wake be of tears and blood. Thus the welcome due "strangers" arose as obligation, because the people of Israel themselves were once strangers at a gate. And the Egyptian keepers of the gate had reduced their victims to a worse plight than that of strangers: they were captives, enslaved. And the gate was thrice bolted against liberation.

~

The prayer concludes: in effect, "may all come to the truth of God and of one another." Surely, placing such a prayer on dynastic lips (". . . in this temple which I have built") has a wrenching irony attached. Solomon and David have been marked by no visible attachment to "strangers." Indeed, their ideology toward such has been, in effect (dare one set it down?), Egyptian. At home they created an equivalent slave population. And abroad they slaughtered with abandon.

~

Strange. On the one hand, obsessive god-talk; on the other, a bloody, contrary spirit: "Your name, your name . . ." The talk, but hardly the walk. What is uttered as a pietism falls to incantation, inviting mimicry and mockery. In the street theater of Jeremiah we shall witness both, and on his lips the mantra, the incantation of magic: ". . . temple of the LORD, temple of the LORD!"

A further point, and a fascinating one. The nations of the world, in the purview of the prayer, are one day to become "like thy people Israel." Referred to are diverse periods of history: a time of unalloyed grandeur, and a time of chastening.

In the first period, that of Solomon, the self-understanding of king and people is heavily beclouded. In the second, suffering and humiliation bring a modest and (to a degree) truthful mind.

To a degree only, alas. It would seem properly biblical to petition the Almighty that all people arrive at truth — especially the truth that no one is to be accounted a "stranger"!

And a different matter entirely, to implore that all peoples become "like us." Alas, in the prayer it stands unqualified, an ostentatious absolute: "become like us," whatever the circumstance, whatever the moral estate of "us."

Are such as we, then, in no need of conversion of heart?

~

A personal note. As children in a Catholic community, we heard for years a concluding prayer of Sunday Mass offered "for the conversion of Russia." There was never an implication that a prayer "for the conversion of America" was in order. Something entirely different was implied: we implored that a benighted people might "become like us."

In those same years, Padre Pio, the Italian monk and mystic, was asked to comment on "the conversion of Russia." His response: "Yes,

Russia will be converted. However, Russia will teach the United States a lesson in conversion."

~

Let us mistrust big words, and big projects likewise. And when the big project has a big word attached, mistrust doubly. To wit: something known as "evangelization" buzzes about Catholic ears these days. Are we to translate thus: "May all come to the truth — especially the truth that no one is 'a stranger'"?

Or is the big word meant to imply the cast of a big net, that others be snared to "become like us"?

In the Catholic community, the phrase has a marked air of absurdity as the year 2007 concludes. We Americans are stuck in a quagmire of adhesive horror: war, pillaging, killing of the innocent. And in the church: cover-up, payola, contempt for victims, protection of predators, unaccountability, misuse of power, scapegoating. These are the marks of defaulting leaders of church and state. A male clerical culture is ill, if not terminally ill. The leaders of the empire likewise. A toxic culture, a toxic church. And multitudes of the innocent must pay.

~

Our text offers warlike proclivities and warrior prayers, together with a religion that enforces the first while uttering the second.

Then, two centuries after Solomon, the exile in Babylon will bring a harsh chastening, as noted above. Eventually the nation will be restored. And the insistence is renewed: outsiders once more are to be made welcome. Indeed, the welcome itself will be a hallmark of restoration.

But the outcome is otherwise, as the Bible testifies: not everyone is made welcome. If there are no strangers, there are certainly enemies. And enemies so awful that warring against them becomes a sanctified undertaking, a crusade.

~

The curiously amputated prayer of Solomon goes on. Grant us to make war "in whatever direction you may send us."

What a god is invoked! No question of a God who would have us make peace "in whatever direction You may send us." War, alas, inflames the blood. Bloodletting in the blood. (In the blood of the god?)

It is in our blood, in the blood of our gods as well. From the era of Solomon until this our day.

~

Prime time, prime occasion. The prayer of Solomon goes thusly: If we, the chosen, have the wit and wisdom to turn our faces toward Jerusalem, on whatever crusade or campaign ("you send us"), then surely you, our god, will vindicate our cause. It is your own.

The prayer takes its stand squarely — in the realm, one thinks, of magical incantation, the murky pseudo-spiritual realm native to war. More exactly, native to warmongering religion. The sentiment is darkly instructive; so is the setting in which it is uttered. The newly built temple is the habitation of the god of war. Solomon makes no bones of it; the edifice is consecrated as such.

~

The Tyrant
This is the festival; we will inter hope
with appropriate mourning. Come, my people.
We will celebrate the massacre of the multitudes.
Come, my people.
I have caused the ghost city known as Limbo
to be inhabited. I have liberated you
from night and from day. . . .
I have decreed death to vision;
all eyes have been excised.
I have sent all dreams to the gibbet. . . .

Mine is the new religion, the new morality.
Mine are the new laws, and a new dogma.

From now on the priests in God's temple
will touch their lips to the hands of idols.

53

Proud men, tall as cypress trees, will bend
to lick the dwarves' feet, and taste the clay.
On this day all over earth the door of beneficent deeds is bolted.
Every gate of prayer throughout heaven is slammed shut today.

Faiz Ahmed Faiz

~

8:46-51　In the short span of five verses, we read these: a mellifluous petition (a later insertion), a historical summary, and a plea.

And so revealing, the prayer. It echoes the heartbroken grief of exile, a long sigh, and tears. And we are bewildered: How to make sense of such words, placed on the lips of a triumphant hierophant-king?

They did not issue from his lips. The words surpass him utterly. We have a stroke of literary genius, the irony of an omniscient witness, risen from the dust and rubble of exile. The prayer belongs to an unknown seer of the quality of a Jeremiah. For a start, almost as an aside, the terrible chastisement of Babylon has brought a sobering truth home: "There is no one without sin."

It was Moses who first said it, drove it home like a nail in the flesh. From the prophets we shall hear it again and again: "Then, 'May they return to themselves in the hostile land where you have deported them.'"

The oppositions hold firm, the bitter wisdom.

~

Let it be noted: For all the fanfare of temple dedication, this is the sequence of things to come, the events hidden from those who witness the Great Day.

First, to the present, and the immediate achievement. The desert years have ended. The people are settled in; the imperial city is built; the chosen dwell content in the shadow of the temple. All seems well, glorious; they raise in praise the cup of David, inebriating, bracing, a vintage of achievement. Praise to our god, praise to ourselves.

~

Nonetheless, one day, something awful will come to pass. The vintage will sour to a gall. The cup will be cast to the ground, shattered. The

54

chosen will be cut off from one another, from the neighbor, from the "stranger." Spiritually they will drift off course, exiled from the truth of life. The glory story ends, not with a bang, but with a whimper.

And what of the king and bureaucrats and generals and priests, they and their grand design? Beneficiaries of the era of glory — did they teach a religion of repentance and creaturehood?

Could the king have composed and uttered such a prayer as stands in the text?

~

Came the final act of the drama. Disaster fell: the great city was leveled, the temple sacked. It was terrible — and it was befitting, as the prophets outrageously insisted. The proud edifice, lauded and blessed in the days of Solomon — "which I have built for your name" — degraded, fell to an abomination. God, Ezekiel tells us, fled the premises (Ezek. 11:23). Justice, peace, welcome accorded victims and strangers — these were disconnected from ritual.

An enemy assaulted and prevailed, terribly. Tenantless, a void, the temple was ground to rubble. The elite of Jerusalem were reduced to a displaced horde, driven afar, subject to the whim and whip of their captors.

~

And in exile, at long last, they came to themselves. They repented of greed and the sorry misuses of royal ego. They forgot to hate — even their captors. Eventually they recalled a few home truths, long neglected. This, for one: "Did not our ancestors endure the like before, in Egypt, that furnace of iron?"

Remembering, they were healed. In exile and enslavement a new social identity was forged, a newborn sense of one another and of God. Babylon, that harsh preceptor! Ezekiel joined the fate of his people, and raised to their lips a wine of bitter wisdom.

~

"It is you who have set them apart as your heritage, as you declared through your servant Moses. . . ."

55

Can a people keep memory intact, alive and life-giving, a sense of being "set apart"? And all the while, compassionate, will they welcome the "stranger at the gate"? A difficult and delicate balance, seldom achieved in practice.

~

Hardly ever achieved, at least in this awful century, our own. The sense of being "set apart" wins out; its forum is a virulent nationalism. The stranger, far from being declared welcome, is set adrift or stigmatized or imprisoned. S(he) need be guilty of no crime. Those newly arrived, seeking sanctuary or fleeing for their lives, are simply declared "undocumented." A culture of contempt speaks through draconian law, to wit: this stranger is unknown, possibly a terrorist — or simply threatens to impede our good life.

8:55-66

King Solomon, we are reminded, is also a high priest — at least for the duration of the Day of Days. His prayer ends. There remains only the bestowal of a blessing. Or rather, the petition of a blessing from the newly installed god.

Again, timing is crucial. Can one imagine a chastened Solomon, summoning the blessing? Alas, a great king, host of a magniloquent occasion, does not easily don sackcloth or utter a prayer that tastes of ashes in the mouth. Solomon never attained such chastening as the prayer implies.

~

". . . observing your law and keeping your commands, as at present . . ."

A nice twist at the end. "Observing law" (in a circumscribed devotional way) admits of no embarrassment in the legacy of David.

Yet one ponders; the litany of crime is not so easily disposed of. It reverberates in the mind: wars of the first and second generations of imperial history, trickery and betrayal, forced labor, burdensome taxation, perquisites seized. In sum, a hardly picayune matter: massive, institutionalized injustice.

56

~

And what of guilt or responsibility? For the occasion, nothing of these shows face. Instead, lofty rhetoric and self-congratulation swarm like a cloud of wasps.

An uneasy conjunction, to be sure, of contradictions and outright absurdities. They will not long hold firm.

~

Solomon's Day. And a week of imperial glory follows. The people exult, "joyous and of good heart." Yahweh, one imagines, is all beatific smiles.

And yet, and yet. Are termites at work in the temple's beams and rafters — and in the palace as well?

The Tyrant and the Convenient Deity (Ch. 9)

We are plunged bewilderingly into a tangle of diverse events. A rather threatening epiphany of the temple god is followed by a veritable firestorm of imperial activity. Only imagine: construction, legislation of corvée, wheeling and dealing with imperial neighbors, setting up and stationing a professional army.

And a hardly small matter — massacres. In the interstices of those famous "laws and ordinances," allowances lurk for sinister behavior.

The impression is strong: two stories, seemingly unrelated (the divine apparition and the imperial projects), are juxtaposed.

"For our instruction"? With access to more forthright texts, we pause over the implication here — that the works and pomps of the king go forward under divine warrant. Thus it is recorded: the god grants an epiphany to his servant Solomon.

~

But wait. Short and sobering, the Week of Glory. Once it has passed, the divine mood alters. Annoyance succeeds éclat. The god is pleased to deliver a monologue. He affirms once more favor from above; retained are the fondest memories of "your father David, innocent of heart and just."

We have heard it before. Astonishing. A spoliative ancestor becomes an icon of rectitude. His son is instructed to gaze, admire, and conduct his life accordingly.

We too gaze, our moral sense shaken. Right or wrong we may be, but we recall a less savory David than the one commended.

Still, the message. Behave in accord with your famous father.

Then a threat. Measure up. Or else.

Solomon's Yahweh — what a deity, what a thick pentimento of ego is laid on the divine physiognomy. And we stand far distant from true God, hearing only the voice of a god.

~

A suggestion. We are urged in our own era to take note of a contrast, and grow wise. Wise in this understanding: imperial authorities create gods to their own image.

No images! Is this the command? No strange gods before me? But in what ethical respect does the accepted god differ from those forbidden "others"?

~

Awful, all but beyond credence, are the depredations of the Sun King. And each is legitimated on high. His religious credentials intact, Solomon briskly moves to confront a key issue: "national security." He reduces to slavery any "foreign elements" within the confines of Israel — tribes who somehow or other survived the sword of his ancestors. Five peoples are mentioned by name.

The "stranger at the gate" accorded welcome? (A blistering welcome — the first "Patriot Act" of our Bible?)

~

The historian hastens to add a kind of pseudo-mitigation, to wit: the king never treats his own subjects thus. Instead, male Israelites are inducted into "his fighting force." An elevation of sorts?

Whatever its import, the assertion was contradicted earlier, when the building of the temple was underway.

~

Turned tyrant (a slight turn, all said), Solomon strikes out, far and wide. No suspect is safe or exempt. Wherever the imperial gaze falls, whether on subjects, citizens of the realm, strangers at the gate, foreigners — all such distinctions are rendered null and void. Each and all are grist for the mills of the god.

~

Our king, as we learned before, is also a sedulous priest. As such, his peccadillos are annually expunged. At the Pasch, at Pentecost, and in time of harvest, he dons sacred robes and mounts the altar to placate the god. Need it be added that such pieties hardly set him on a different course, bringing compunction or compassion?

O convenient deity, servant of the most high Solomon!

~

"It goes on happening and will happen again," writes the poet Rozewicz Tadeusz.

No. It will not, not forever. Soon, Isaiah and his like, embattled and majestic, will appear on the desolate scene and thunderously speak up.

And eventually Jesus will be born of this hapless line of godlings, David and Solomon. And we dare say it, and believe it: Nothing will be the same, ever again.

From Solomon to Jeroboam: Kings Run Amok

(Chs. 10–13)

Turning and turning in the widening gyre,
The falcon cannot hear the falconer.
Things fall apart; the center cannot hold. . . .

W. B. Yeats

The King and the Queen:
Wisdom Compounded, Unconfounded (10:1-13)

At first glance the story might be thought no more than a charming diversion, enriching the literal, the deadly factual, with a nimbus of glory.

Still, go slow. No biblical episode yields its meaning to a first glance.

To our scene, then. "Mine eyes have seen the glory. . . ." Behold Solomon in midlife, riding high, a celestial-terrestrial portent, glory and riches attending.

And one day there arrives at his court a mysterious "other," a woman unlike any among his domestic loves. She is a queen in her own right, an equal.

~

Her person, her aura, her legend! These have awakened resonances in other times and cultures. Thus in the Koran the queen is named Bilqis, and among Ethiopian Christians, Makeda. Coming together in our tale are elements that elsewhere, most conspicuously in the Moslem faith, are considered serious and precious in the telling.

~

Assyrian records of the 8th-7th centuries mention five Arabian queens by name, which furnishes a curious and revealing parallel to this feminine domination.

John L. McKenzie, *Dictionary of the Bible*

~

In our version the queen walks under seven veils, unnamed, peerless, an image of beauty and mystery.

Why then the story? What is its point in the fabulous court of Solomon? Does our text hint ever so subtly of a spiritual void, of royal needs as yet unmet?

All to the contrary (that first glance again). We are assured that great Solomon has ready access to the cornucopia of creation, tipping to his least touch. Is he not emperor par excellence, king of kings, greatly surpassing his father?

In the Davidic dynasty, the material splendors of court and temple surpass all others. And in this Sun King, the royal line shines in apogee.

~

Let us skip the glory-be, pondering the nemesis. One day Solomon will proceed to pull the house down upon his head. Mightily he will pull glory down, and a liverish, regressive tyrant will emerge. He will forsake the temple god, turning instead to worship Astarte, deity of his concubines.

Still, dolorous events lie mercifully in the future. Meantime, the chosen people walk in a summer of content. Some of them.

And high noon, even for the fortunate, is fleeting and frail.

~

The weather is springlike, mild and gracious. And a fanfare sounds on the air. A glorious intervention! A queen arrives from afar, accompanied by habiliments of beauty and power. Let the superlatives proliferate "like sun-starts on a stream."

She is fabulously wealthy, of surpassing fame; in all the world her equal does not exist. No one her peer? She arrives to prove, or have disproved, the surpassing glory and intellect of the fabled king. A spiritual quest drives her. Her "very great train" is the setting, the foil that reflects facets of a jewel-set purpose. She comes in search of wisdom.

~

Fascinating. The queen enters a scene bathed in a haze of gold.

Why then this epiphany? What does the queen bring to Solomon the supreme?

Of the king we know a great deal, not entirely to his honor. Of the queen of Sheba we know practically nothing. Nothing of her forebears, her culture, the forces that brought accession to power.

Only this is told: Solomon traded in gold, spices, and precious stones with her people, the Yemenites of our day. Was her errand no more than a prosaic trade mission? So it would seem. Still, even if reluctantly, fact must yield to myth.

~

The queen too is wise, we are told. She is impelled toward Jerusalem by rumors of a ruler of unmatched wisdom. The stories lead her like a star. She must encounter him, no matter the distance or impediment.

So it was done. Glorious as a sunrise, she arrives at the court of the Sun King.

The story, we note, is placed within the wider ambiance of the rise and fall of Solomon. The setting seems deliberate, a pause, a mitigation. It is as though a peerless inner freedom were being offered the unfree.

A golden dungeon, and she bearing the key?

~

The king, we are told, need seek for nothing; excess, consumption, and accumulation are the hallmarks of his court. But let us take a closer look. Our Bible is no acolyte or apologist of imperialists. Quite the contrary: its intent is cannily subversive of such.

Solomon, as presented, is sunken deep in time and this world. A "dweller upon the earth"? Have time and this world laid claim to him, an iron hand clapped to his shoulder? Do honors and emoluments weigh heavy? Is he unfree, even unhappy? Might he not yield to longings, learn to breathe free in the presence of the queen from afar?

~

In regard to her, no such questions arise. She is lightsome of spirit, unentailed. She traverses the world; her voyages win an ever greater measure of freedom. She possesses what she seeks; she seeks a deeper measure of what she possesses.

What well, what tradition, does she drink from? Of this we know nothing.

From afar, rumor sends her in search; she senses that Solomon too drinks from a well of wisdom.

Common source, one thinks — and diverse run.

~

The queen is an Edenic figure, an epiphany granted on the moment — then vanished. It is as though she were born this morning, fully adult and accoutered, indentured to no power on earth.

Our text omits much, and thereby enriches speculation. Nothing, it would seem, impedes the single-minded search of the queen — no heavy military, economic, diplomatic, religious trappings, roles, expectations — such concerns (obsessions?) as preoccupy the king and furrow his brow.

~

The sequence leading to her story is cunningly instructive. Immediately before the arrival of the queen, we were told in some detail of the king's constructions in Jerusalem, of his vast armaments and military campaigns.

All that heavy-duty, clanking prose!

Abruptly, a sea change, a glorious interlude. The queen is announced and her visit commences.

Then she departs. And a void opens. It is as though wisdom vanished with her. And a catalogue begins, wearyingly, of Solomon's vast riches.

~

Riches. What are true riches? The presence of the queen has provoked the question, even as her detachment from wealth offers a hint.

Who is truly rich, the king or the queen? As presented, her wealth is untainted; it has no history. And his? Dark the story, the royal bloodline, the unspeakable crimes of seizure.

~

In this personage, has Solomon encountered his equal or, dare one venture, his superior? Whatever her eminence, the queen takes it for granted.

Never has such a woman stood in the king's presence. In his adult years he has known only nameless concubines and a number of foreign wives. The latter are politically important to him, but they are powerless to heal his slowly hardening heart. A showcase of sexual fantasy and satisfaction, little or nothing more.

~

Poetry governs the days together of the king and his royal guest:

The queen
communed
with him

of all
that was

in
her
heart.

The emphasis is on her, an easy though urgent candor. It is implied that the king — all animus, male, dominant — has great need of this communing. At some length, she speaks of "what is in her heart." And a veil is drawn; we are not privy to the subjects entered upon.

The king responds. A profound mutuality is set humming between them. His mind is refreshed by hers, the anima mundi. His weapons and wealth, his diplomacies and wars and dark-browed brooding above the chessboard of power — these for the moment are set aside.

Under that male armor, that layered cloth of gold, what organ beats? A heart? Yes. A needy heart, weighed down.

At length his heart takes voice, sings. He is literally heartened by her presence; he grows attentive and falls to rest.

～

For her part, she purposes to view the wonders of the court, whether material or spiritual. Quite the woman of the world! The king proposes a tour of temple and palace. They walk and converse.

Quiet takes over. The queen grows speechless with awe. His riches, his wisdom are far greater than their worldwide echo:

The half
was not

told
me;

your wisdom
and prosperity

exceed
the fame

of which I
heard.

～

She is an innocent. Does she question nothing — the source of the king's treasures, the sanguinary wars, the plunder and loot?

Of these skeletons, bones, dry bones, she hears not a mutter or a rattle. It is as though she assumed her friend to be innocent as herself; as
though she saw no blood on his hands — or on his gold. Yet, beyond
doubt, a man of blood he is.

~

Innocence creates its kind. Instinctively admiring the queen, her child-
like candor, Solomon tastes, for the moment, a kind of primal innocence.

A hint, even, of a closer union? Does she seek to prolong the visit,
perhaps even to become a member of his entourage? Or perhaps she
speaks of what he cannot, disjoined as he is from the common life, ar-
mored against the poetry of life.

All that wisdom! Nonetheless, he is clumsy and inarticulate in matters of the heart. His world is hard-edged, abrasive, rigid, all boundary
and bone, occluded from the curve and swirl, the dance of life.

He weighs the world like an ingot of gold — his gold, to be sure. What
price? Everything — everyone — worth such and such. Or worthless.

No one lends him skills of poetry and song to fill an emotional void;
no one relieves the leaden prose of existence.

In the company of this woman a longing rises in him. For what? For
the balm of the feminine to lave his parched soul? She hints at a proffer;
she will help.

~

The imbalance of the king's soul is more than discommoding; it is
dangerous. He and his warriors and counselors are only partially awake
— to reality, to truth, to their rightful place in the larger world. Ignorant
or contemptuous of the feminine, usurping half the human tribe as their
"possession," they stalk the world, owners of others. Of others as
"things."

They are governed by an image woefully awry, and they behave in accord with the image. It is as though, in their benighted view, they com-
prised and exhausted the human, these warriors and schemers, ignorant
amid weapons and wars, ungovernable appetites hurling about the
world.

We know them; we have seen them in our lifetime. Killers, possessed by their possessions. Possessed by a cult of "more." And thus, save for some intervention or grace, they live and die. Their prime exemplars rule America in these years of war upon war.

They would rule the world. And the world trembles.

Welcome to the Pentagon, one of the world's most famous buildings. As home of the nation's military, it is an internationally recognized symbol of American power and influence. It is from within these walls, housing the headquarters of the Department of Defense, that military forces are deployed worldwide to protect American interests and to promote democracy [sic]. . . .

The Pentagon provides the command and control facilities that enable the U.S. military to be the most efficient and powerful in the world.

From the Pentagon tourist brochure

~

On April 13, '01, Good Friday, six members of Atlantic Life Community poured their blood on nine pillars of the River Entrance. . . .

Despite a 25-year history of such witnesses, Pentagon security forces were not prepared for the action. . . .

Art Laffin, *Catholic Worker*

~

Let it be said plain. The predicament of Solomon is endemic to his kind. The king's court, for all its decor and pomp, is deviant from true order, an enclave of destructors.

The scheming and killing and amassing of riches bring on a profound stupor of the heart. How shall they shake off such ways?

The queen, we note, has no quarrel with the grandiose Solomonic sway. And yet her style is a subtle argument against his. Presuming Solomon to be as innocent as herself, she grants him a great gift — an unaccustomed innocence, a sip at her well. He drinks, lifts his head, and for a time his sight clears. He sees the world through her eyes. For the nonce, relief and respite are his.

And his gift to her? It is left in general terms:

... everything
she
desired

and
asked
for.

~

She enters his heart, transforming him through praise (one thinks, largely undeserved praise). She goes further, partaking of his religion, praising his god.

This is an extraordinary leap. Does she know that the god of Solomon is the creation of Solomon, an imperial self-image? If she knows, she cares not a whit. Her logic is simple, a matter of the heart. If the king is admirable, so must be the king's god. Admirable, whether the god be named Yahweh or Astarte or Baal.

What the king reveres, she shall revere. Why not? Hers is the logic of innocence. She stakes no claims. Praise for his god is free of self-interest. Thus the doxology uttered by the queen —

Blessed
be

the lord
your god,

who
has delighted

in
you ...

— is hardly to be taken as evidence that she has come to the "true faith." (In any case, no such faith is at hand.) Thus her praise of the temple god

as the providential source of Solomon's authority must be read as heavy
with irony:

God
has made

you
king,

to maintain

law
and
justice.

It may have been so; the mandate may have been so worded. But it
has been grievously violated — as we have seen before, as will be dramatized again after the queen's departure.

∽

On the face of it, her visit marks an ecstatic hiatus, a moment. A moment of grace? Under her gaze, it is as though shadows fled the high noon
of Jerusalem. No dark side of glory; only the sun at apogee, days of wine
and roses. . . .
And yet, and yet.

∽

The grace of her presence fades from Jerusalem. She sails off; a perfume fills her sails. And Solomon? He resumes his Solomonic ways. Alert
to the main chance, he will shortly discover that the temple deity has un-
dergone a change of mood. The god glowers, he (sic) grows darkly critical
of his quondam darling.
Forthwith the king will shuck off responsibility in favor of a coven of
other, more responsive idols, Astarte and Baal. From one idol to many —
no large step.

∽

The queen departs; the king regresses. Still, our story lingers in the mind — an odor, faint but unmistakable, of flowers pressed within the pages of a venerable text.

The king's degradation follows, then shortly, his ruin. Yet lucky we, who have witnessed, if only for a time, an exquisite "coincidentia oppositorum," have heard the gentle "clash of ironies," a clapper striking a golden bell.

It rings slowly — hardly joyfully. Like the memory of joy. Like a bell of passing?

The Great King: Possessed by Possessions (10:14-29)

Her majesty has departed. Male, warrior, appetitive consumer, Solomon stands once more at center stage. And without prelude, we are ushered into a rather vulgar tour of the king's treasure trove.

Something implied? Perhaps our historian is also a moralist?

The mordantly possessive eye of the king ranges about his trove. Are we being offered an oblique instruction? To wit: nothing of these riches avails, whether toward contentment, integrity of conscience, or conduct. Nothing toward the relief or well-being of the king's people. Quite the opposite.

Remarkable, awful: the plight of his subjects in the face of the anointing, in view of the honor purportedly paid (but, truth told, with a cursory bow) "justice and the law."

It is as though Solomon brushed a cobweb from the royal countenance. "Justice, the law"? These scarcely signify. Amassing, computing, and showcasing his riches are the main tasks at hand. And we note the vulgarity, the frivolous excess. Everything is aimed at a show of military prowess — "shields of gold, bucklers of beaten gold" — or of imperial ego — "a throne of ivory and gold, lions and bulls rampant, the seat elevated by six steps."

Excess, decadence, a mind grown parched and dingy. How wisdom has fled! Like one struck blind, how far he has wandered from the moment long ago, when he resolved the conflict of the two outcast women and their infants living and dead.

Now commerce and the military, those hyphenated realities, consume his attention. The royal fleets sail off and return, teeming with wealth.

10:26-29

And the king "collected chariots and drivers" by the thousands. "Collected" indeed. Drivers and chariots — possessions on a par with ingots of gold. Or, for that matter, with wives.

The military forces, we are told, were distributed among garrison cities, a line of territorial defense, a permanent armed force. The latter, prior to his rule, was unheard of in Israel.

Canny Solomon! He stations chariots and drivers strategically, to protect trade routes of the Red Sea. The show of force is aimed at averting an improbable — indeed, all but unimaginable — assault. His aim falls short. The bristling precautions lead, straight as an arrow to a bull's eye, to disaster.

Shadows over the Empire (11:1-8)

Our historian places on the king's foreign wives a heavy burden: we are told that the women occasion the king's apostasy. According to official history, these wives introduced foreign deities to Jerusalem: Astarte of Canaan, Milcom of the Ammonites, Chemosh of Moab. Under such baleful influence the heart of the king turned away from the temple god, the "true" god.

~

It may appear from the preceding that the commentator is inclined to distrust this version of the Royal Decline and Fall. The rot was underway earlier: royal misbehavior. It is our contention that Solomon was an idolater from the start. The vast, costly construction of temple and palace, the corvée, the taxation, the bureaucratic sycophants, and worst of all, the wars — taken together, these indicate a massive violation of the king's original charge and vocation: to honor "justice and equity."

~

Solomon, for all his pieties, is a "dweller upon the earth." As the queen reminded him (and all in vain), he was anointed to honor "justice and equity" in the land. Instead, he "worships the works of his hands." He tossed his heart on a scales and sold it for meat. Heartless, his rule turned to iron.

~

And what of the god of the royal temple? We have suggested naming him a royal projection, a mirror image. As such, the deity either colludes with or remains indifferent to royal derelictions.

And what of those famous "commands and ordinances" enjoined on the king? These simply exert no weight on his social contract, on matters of "justice and equity." Royal religion is a different matter entirely: sanctuary decor, rubrical niceties. In plain denial of the law set down in Deuteronomy, the Solomonic ethic gravely affects the fate of "widows and orphans and strangers at the gate," worsening misery, multiplying grief.

~

Other matters intrude and win attention, win the day. Kept close is the handbook of feasts and fasts, of bowing and scraping in the great sanctuary. And in the world at large, anything goes: self-interest, greed, violence. Solomon has scuttled the original covenant, the solemn and sublime compact that incised social justice on tablets of stone, that insistently joined matters of justice to integrity of worship.

We have seen it at length, the high-flown futility, the blindness. Along with architectural follies, Solomon built national systems whose mortar and blocks were injustice and violence. Thus he polluted the temple worship and invited social disaster.

~

An old story, and a new. To our own day it is never done with. Greed and violence proliferate; class lines are sharply drawn. American culture comprises a knot of the rapacious super-rich, an embattled middle class, and multitudes of the impoverished and homeless. On which sector the politics fawns, and whom it chooses to ignore — these require no elaborating.

Today, an ominous millennium roils the world. In the United States a security superstate takes form; the "Patriot Act" gives ominous notice. To keep the uneasy peace, "chariots and charioteers" are deployed in great numbers throughout the nation and the world, restive with misery and ecological degradation. To keep foreign enemies at bay (even purported or imagined enemies), a vast permanent military force is deployed on land, sea, and air. Add to this fleets, world markets, NAFTA, the multicorporate seizures. A Solomonic hegemony, in sum:

> The king had a fleet of Tarshish ships at sea. . . . Once every three years the fleet of Tarshish ships would come with a cargo of gold, silver, ivory, apes, and monkeys.

~

Enemies and Traitors: The Decline and Fall (11:9-43)

On the once fair and far-reaching realm, an icy season descends, a winter of discontent. The mood is reflected in the temple god. He too feels the weather to the bone: short cold days and long cold nights. Cold dark thoughts and words are uttered.

Then the empire divides in two, like a fruit gone rotten.

After the fact, the dire scission, something famously known as the will of Yahweh is of course invoked. That will has grown fractious, aroused by the encroachment of other deities. From the temple, the threat of catastrophe rumbles away: ". . . but for the sake of your father David, not in your lifetime."

One is led to wonder yet again: What special virtue of David has merited delay of judgment?

As god, so the votary? We adjudged David, even according to the official record, a man of blood who honored neither friend nor principle. And as to consequence of crime, an artful dodger indeed.

Like father, like son? Withdrawn, capricious, hedonistic, Solomon grows old. He "rules" in a vacuum of power, from a throne of ivory and gold, "six steps" above it all, remote from people and event.

Prior to the onset of ruinous events, our historian has been careful to convey the illusion of an empire intact. Subtly ironic, he presented the reign through Solomon's eyes, the unalloyed glory and triumph.

~

Then disaster looms. Shadows dog the king's steps.

They were short at first, the shadows, hardly worth notice, easily brushed aside. Yet, and yet, they were there, and irked, and walked with him. Even at the start of his long reign, Solomon could exert only a sporadic, partial control over segments of his empire.

Blood will have blood, generation to generation. Saul, then David set the awful law in place. Blood came due; the law descended like a blade, slitting the artery of empire. There was set loose a torrent — hateful, vengeful memory. Time passed. Solomon was engulfed.

Rivals, enemies, the envious long ignored — these buzzed away, like a nest of wasps mortised to the walls of temple and palace. The cloud of stingers rose, buzzing into midair. Enemies abroad, betrayal at home.

David had created hostilities outside his borders. He lived to endure the betrayal of his son Absalom. Enemies and traitors were his dire bequest to Solomon. The sin was made original once more. Laceration of spirit befell. Thus. A certain Jeroboam "was in service to Solomon and rebelled against him."

We are appalled, and instructed as well.

11:26-43

One hardly knows whom to judge the more abominable: Solomon and his encampments of slave labor, his fleets and chariots — or this young rising star, Jeroboam, this "man of means," an "industrious young man."

He bides his time, cultivating the king, who in full-rigged folly "put him in charge of the forced labor of two entire tribes, comprising the house of Joseph."

What a task! One thinks: two rogues, each serving and deserving the other.

For his part, the temple god abruptly changes sides, apparently joining with the rebel Jeroboam. Then a dramatic encounter, and a stunning mime. A prophet, unpronounceably named Ahijah, encounters Jeroboam on a road outside Jerusalem. In presence of the renegade, Ahijah tears his cloak in twelve parts, dramatically underscoring an oracle — and rendering it certain to be verified.

The oracle is verbose; its purport is a summary of divine resentments, heretofore often aired. To wit: Yahweh is furious with Solomon. The king has overreached himself. Breakup of the realm is immanent. Ten portions of the cloak are handed over to Jeroboam; rather than a son of the incumbent, he will reign in Israel.

The Seamless Cloak, Torn (Ch. 12)

The old pattern repeats itself. Absalom turned on his father; now, hard upon the death of Solomon, his son Rehoboam mounts the throne. This worthy will prove no relief from his father. The son is hard as adamantine, stubborn as the royal mule he goads along. In mercy or compassion he has no part.

All Israel assembles for the proclamation of the new king. It is a scene of unexpected tenderness, a revelation as well of the dark legacy of the Sun King. The people are bowed to earth under a burden of taxes, corvée, and poverty. Their plea is a poetry of pathos, a generational plaint.

They also make a proffer:

Your father
laid

on us
a heavy yoke.

If you
lighten

the harsh
service . . .

imposed
on us,
we
will
serve
you.

Playing for time, Rehoboam sends them away. He consults the elders. They also counsel compassion:

If
you

will be
the servant

of
this
people . . .

Rehoboam spurns them. An unbending fool, he turns to his cronies. Like their leader, they dream dark dreams and move to inhabit them. An impenetrable phalanx of power is forming.

What course shall this malfeasant take? Shortly, brutally, we are informed. The image is of a stark inhumanity. Tell the people this: The poetry, the plaints are canceled. This is brutal prose, a pronunciamento of doom:

My little finger is thicker than my father's loins. My father put a heavy yoke on you, I will weigh it heavier. My father beat you with whips, I will beat you with scorpions.

The threat is launched; absolute domination is the goal.

~

Bush to Formalize a Defense Policy of Hitting First.
Plans on Iraq Intensify.
President Bush has directed his top national security aides to make a doctrine of pre-emptive action against states and terrorist groups trying to develop weapons of mass destruction into the foundation of a new national security strategy. . . .

Iraq is clearly first on the target list for such action, and already the CIA and the defense department have stepped up efforts

to unseat Saddam Hussein in a last effort to avoid the necessity of
a full-scale invasion. . . .

New York Times, 17 June 2002

~

A thoroughgoing tyrant, Rehoboam knows little and cares less for
his people's well-being. For the restive northerners, in shaky alliance with
Judah, he cares (need it be said?) nothing at all.

Unity is ripped to shreds. Years before, the prophet tore his cloak,
speaking darkly of things to come: the death of Solomon, the breakup of
the seemingly seamless empire.

Here and now, strike. The Israelis have had enough of tyranny, and
more than enough. To the war tents!

~

In contempt or outright provocation, Rehoboam is past master. He
dispatches a certain Adoram to oversee the forced labor crews in the
north. The behavior of the henchman is beyond bearing; he is shortly
stoned to death.

~

From bad to worse. The exiled Jeroboam has returned from Egypt
and is crowned king of divided Israel. A political animal, he senses a danger to his hegemony. The peril lurks in an ancient custom: for generations the people have made an annual pilgrimage outside their own (pres-
ently his own) territory, wending their way to the temple in Jerusalem.

With a jerk of the reins, he halts the custom in its tracks. Why not
our shrine, on our own land? Why not indeed?

And more. In Egypt he had seen golden calves set up and worshiped.
Why not the like here, among us? So, ruinously, it was done.

~

Historians suggest that the decree was not of itself an act of apostasy.
The images of young, vigorous bulls — these might have been intended
as icons of the attributes of Yahweh, visible signs of invisible presence.

Still, a dangerous precedent is set. Beyond the borders of Israel, such images bear ominous, forbidden overtones: they symbolize worship of the Baals.

A heavy doubt arises: Can the proposal of Jeroboam be sound? Can Yahwism be restored by veneration of ambiguous, quasi-pagan forms?

Perhaps he has forgotten the golden calf of Sinai (Exod. 32:4)?

~

He is hardly apt to forget. Cleverly, he links the calf image with the liberation from Egypt. Let them borrow the image from the same land: "Here is your god, O Israel, who brought you out of the land of Egypt!"

~

In the pagan setting of Egypt, the calf images proposed by Jeroboam are rife. And in Jerusalem, as throughout the land, images of the divinity are sternly outlawed. The bulls thunder into a forbidden landscape.

Is this the crushing irony, that Egypt has come home to the city of David and Solomon?

Woe to one who introduces ambiguous images! Nothing daunted, the innovator goes blithely forward. The latent power and intense aura of the images, the implications that cling to them through foreign (and, in principle, forbidden) traditions — he grasps nothing of these.

Jeroboam has dared open a sealed door. Beyond lies a lunar landscape, its people assimilated, disappeared into the pagan leaven.

~

Let it be granted; he is a genius of sorts, this Jeroboam. And for that, the more dangerous. He walks a high wire — safe, at least for a time. Still, a bullish political animal has blundered into the sanctuary; wrong person, wrong place.

Jeroboam is devastatingly detailed and serious. He would set in place the foundations of a "new religion." His tactic goes somewhat like this. Place the ancient customs in a new setting. Let the memories abide, of course; but create a new locale, a new structure to house and anchor them. Let there be a new priesthood even, drawn "from the people who were not Levites."

~

A new setting for the mystery implies the onset of new meaning. It is as though in the Christian era, church authorities were to propose, "We will celebrate Easter, yes, but in Israel-Palestine only." And this with the purpose, covert or not, of an utter change in the purport of the mystery.

What in effect would be the change proposed? Perhaps this: the resurrection of Christ is a purely local, personal conquest of death, a unique "divine" event, with no implication for the "resurrection of the body" of all humans.

~

An adjustment here, a nudge there — Jeroboam tampers with the sacred fabric. He is a supreme pragmatist, distrustful of the hegemony of the old city. The pilgrimage to Jerusalem rankles. His riposte, in effect: Let us seek the god elsewhere. Our people too have, or shortly shall have, a royal sanctuary, processions, our "feast of the eighth month," the celebration of Tents — these together with our own priesthood.

And of the ancient ways, so carefully prescribed, what remains? Little or nothing. Revered memories, places, dates — these are rendered null and void.

~

Changes, changes. Ring the changes!

The fool overreaches, invading sacred spaces, dates, persons, forging questionable images. Contemptuous of the holy, he rushes in where angels . . . One thinks: he resembles his own bull come to life, a despot havocking the sanctuary. And bringing the structure down — on his own head.

~

Nefas! "Procul este!" "Keep thy distance!" is the cry of the Cumaean sibyl against too-close access to mystery. Jeroboam has dared come too close, has violated a great taboo. He goes further. A self-declared high priest, he vests and mounts the altar.

And the rival god of Jerusalem, that jealous ascendancy, is stirred to a fury.

Jeroboam thought to create a rival to Solomon's line, or David's. And he created only a bonfire of the vanities, his own downfall.

No Strange Gods before Me (Ch. 13)

A wonderful story, and awful. The god of Jerusalem, as is known and will shortly be demonstrated once more, is incomparably powerful, firmly installed, artful, dudgenous, finical for due recognition, peevish in face of rivalries. In such qualities and strengths, the deity utterly surpasses this upstart king of Israel, his bulls of metal and his fake priesthood.

The god resolves on a move. First item: that rival altar — it must come down. The denouement is abrupt, and brilliantly recounted. An anonymous "holy man" is dispatched to confront the rival. And a close, tight drama is underway. The envoy arrives at the shrine just as the king-priest is commencing the service. Abruptly, proceedings are halted. The emissary launches a diatribe.

It is as though the stones of the table were a living being. "Altar, altar!" The cry implies both contempt and command. A rhetorical master stroke. On the instant the altar comes mordantly alive.

As for the interloping celebrant, he is ignored, held in contempt.

A dumb artifact of stone is addressed. Jeroboam stands there, dumb and deaf as stone, while the stone table seems endowed with hearing and intelligence.

~

We note a curious historical fact. Verses 2 and 23 are a later addition, announcing the future reform of Josiah, as though his decree were already in place.

Of interest also: precisely worded as to event [2 Kings 23:16-20], and mentioning a proper name, the verses violate the prophetic form; they are reduced to a literal midrash.

~

"Altar, altar!" The bellow of the holy man ricochets off the stone, striking the perpetrator full in the face. Anger and confusion break out.

Jeroboam points to the intruder: "Seize him!" And on the moment, two shocking events. The outstretched arm of the king withers. And the altar explodes, self-destructs. The ashes of the blasphemous sacrifice fall and fall.

～

Is the episode to be thought a vindication of one god against many? Does the god of Jerusalem merit thereby a capital letter and the confession of believers: "true God, no other before Me"?

More: Shall worship be allowed only in the temple of Solomon, and nowhere else? Is faith thus narrowed, by the gimlet eye of a god, to fidelity toward liturgical niceties of time and place?

～

Statements and stories turn and turn about in a grammar of inquiry. It is an old biblical game, enormously helpful, inviting questions unending. This, for instance: If religious fealty in this or that setting fails to awaken a sense of justice and compassion, how shall the worship of one place, Jerusalem, be judged superior to another, that of Bethel?

To put matters crudely: Why does the altar of Bethel explode, and that of Jerusalem stand intact? Does the behavior of Jeroboam in fact differ greatly from that of the champions, favorites, and priests of the central city — from the behavior of Saul, David, Solomon, and their court?

～

And a final, vexed question; it will be raised repeatedly by the prophets. Are such matters as whips and scorpions, heavy yokes laid on the living, forced labor and enslavement, jihads, betrayals, wars of extermination — are these irrelevant to the "religion" of kings, or to our moral evaluation of their works and pomps? Are such issues of no moment to Yahweh?

～

The story of the exploding altar reveals a pattern and conception of "religion," as commonly received. Thus the "holy man" is dispatched to Bethel, gifted with literally explosive powers.

And one is led to think of an errand on which the same holy man is not sent. Indeed, prior to the delicts of Jeroboam, no such messenger was dispatched in reproof of the crimes of Saul, Solomon, or their favorites.

In one instance only — the adultery and murder committed by David — is royal crime adduced and accountability pressed. With that exception, the eminences of our books run amok, wage horrid wars — and emerge, untouched by judgment.

~

For a while, untouched. Only wait. Year, month, week, day, hour, minute of judgment: Tuesday, September 11, 2001, 10:15 A.M.; the World Trade Center, the Pentagon. A circle added to Dante's inferno.

~

The story of the invaded temple at Bethel induces confusion, to say the least, regarding the moral standards of all concerned — the god of Jerusalem, the servant-kings and their entourages.

The deity is honored by fulsome tribute, vast sacrifices. Yet he (sic) remains unpredictable and arbitrary, exerting only the slightest pressure — or none at all — upon the consciences of kings.

No wonder if believers (and scholars as well) are appalled and confused.

~

Confusion is hardly to be thought induced by an ancient text only. To this day we Christians, a people who confess the Incarnation of God in Christ, who confess the verity of his life and death — we love meagerly, obey grudgingly, wage war fervently.

In our century the criminality of David's line is like a moon, fading at dawn of a torrid sun. The crimes of the king pale before our own. The litany of contemporary horrors is endless, boundless. From German gas chambers to Hiroshima, to the wasting wars of Vietnam, Granada, Panama, Cosovo, to South African savageries, to the Stalinist camps, to Somalia and former Yugoslavia and the Gulf wars, to the Central America slaughter, to Northern Ireland, to East Timor, Congo, Sudan, Biafra, to Afghanistan and Iraq — on and on the trail of extermination and betrayal, of tears and blood.

What has befallen our humanity, our purported Christianity?

With due tribute paid the saints and martyrs in our midst, the example of Christ has had as little impact on Christians as the prophets could urge on the behavior of their kings.

~

A counterpoise, a hope. There remains, despite all, the healing reality of Christ, of the martyrs and saints. Never quite done with, never once failing us. Through them, as though in spite of ourselves, we are not utterly lost, not a "massa damnata."

Not lost — summoned, rather. This is our dignity and our burden. A summons has sounded from the tormented lips of Christ: that we raise an outcry, act sanely, resist the principalities of death.

~

I read it here in your very word,
in the story of the gestures
with which your hands cupped themselves
around our becoming — limiting, warm.

You said "live" out loud, and "die" you said lightly,
and over and over again you said "be."
But before the first death came murder.
A fracture broke across the rings you'd ripened.
A screaming shattered the voices

that had just come together to speak you,
to make of you a bridge
across the chasm of everything.

And what they have stammered ever since
are fragments
of your ancient name.

R. M. Rilke

~

Our story veers along, almost of its own will, strangely reluctant to end.

Next chapter, and once more the destroyer of forbidden altars. The man of god, we read, is invited by chastened king Jeroboam to sit, eat, and drink with him, "and I will present you with a gift."

The king seems a shameless schemer, an ancestor strikingly resembling a Herod-to-come; that one, it will be recalled, blundered through Matthew's Gospel, sword drawn. On one occasion, he sought to inveigle the Magi to report to himself concerning "the place where the newborn lies, that I too may come and reverence him." But they evade him by the good offices of an angel, and "return to their homeland by another route" (Matt. 2:1-12).

~

In the present episode, the man of God has small reason indeed to trust this Jeroboam. The invasive messenger has the upper hand; he is stern — and obedient. Yahweh has instructed him not to tarry, to return by another route, a road he (carefully, it would seem, for who might overhear and thwart?) omits mention by name.

Then a complication. There dwells in the area a species of "prophet," an elder, inspired but of lower rank than a "man of God." This one hears of the wonders wrought at the altar of Bethel. Forthwith he sets out in search of the man of God. He overtakes him and repeats the offer of hospitality. And is refused, on the same grounds: Yahweh forbids it.

"Ah, but — "

And one almost sees the venerable hands and eyes raised to heaven. He himself, the elder avers, has received from an angel a contrary word: "bring the man of God to your house, feed and refresh him."

The narrator appends a laconic footnote as to the purported angelic message: "He lied."

For what motive, we are left in the dark, told only this: the man of god ignored the word of god, and went along with the false-hearted one.

And tragedy, admitting no favorites, descends like lightning on the man of God — just as he himself brought ruin on the king. The "crime" was this: he trusted an angel of Yahweh rather than the word of Yahweh. Quite a distinction!

But, but. Given the morality exhibited in the Bible thus far, one finds the delict here to be venial indeed — and the punishment excessive: "Your body will not enter the sepulcher of your ancestors" (13:22).

~

Worse and worse befalls; our folktale is merciless as a Grimm confabulation. On the road the man of god is killed by a lion, and his body lies unburied. The awful news reaches the prophet. Like old Tobit or a "good Samaritan," he arrives — alas, too late to succor the living. Hurriedly he takes up the corpse and buries it in a grave prepared for his own body.

~

And we are reminded of another act of compassion, centuries later. On a day of infamy, Joseph of Arimathea will give his tomb over to a dishonored Corpse: "When evening fell, a wealthy man from Arimathea arrived, Joseph by name. He was another of Jesus' disciples. . . . Taking the body, Joseph wrapped it in fresh linen and laid it in his own new tomb. . . ." (Matt. 27:57, 59-60).

~

The unnamed prophet instructs his sons; at his own death he is to be buried beside the man of God: "For the word he spoke under command of Yahweh will certainly be fulfilled."

A curious tale! Of the source or motive of that famous lie, we are told nothing. And questions proliferate. Did the elder hope to learn something, to inveigle a word regarding himself or the future of Jeroboam? Indeed, why his errand at all? Further, why must an outsider be sent to the city to denounce the evil deeds of the priest-pretender? Did not a prophet already dwell there, aware of the shady liturgies and the altar of contention?

And why did no evil befall this prophet, whose silence is so puzzling (so prudent)? Further, how has he merited the title of prophet, who apparently turns a blind eye on an issue of import to the god of Jerusalem?

~

The episode concludes on a somber note. Jeroboam is apparently wicked beyond reform; he continues his evil practices in the "high places." Ruin and extermination of his line shortly follow.

Great Solomon is no more; all is scission and chaos. The center cannot hold.

Of Kings and Their Gods: A Tale of Woe

(Chs. 14–22)

All great advances have involved illegality.

Bertrand Russell, *Which Way to Peace?*

Jeroboam and Rehoboam: Undone by Idols (Ch. 14)

A terrible story. A tale of disguise and cruelty and the misuse of prophecy in servitude to magic. And of the thwarting of artful Jeroboam by Yahweh. The deity, as anyone knows (and as Jeroboam should have known, this loutish fool), is more clever by far than the canniest of mortals. He (sic) moves faster than the quickest horse on earth, and has at command lightning bolts more awful than Vesuvius, awake and roaring.

This god — one (or Solomon, or his cohorts, the priests) could go on and on. But be sensible. Beware at any cost a confrontation with the testy high and mighty!

~

Also a theme we have heard before. From David's delict to Jeroboam's, it is decreed by the temple god that little children suffer and die for the sins of the mighty.

Jeroboam, we were told, has refused to budge; under no duress or

87

threat will he remove the bronze bulls set up in his rival temple. He also surmises that the prophet Ahijah will prove no friend to him and his images. And this for the simplest of reasons: Jeroboam and his idols are rivals of the great temple of Solomon.

Nonetheless, Jeroboam must face a crisis. His little son is ill, and the future bleak. What to do? The father is out of favor; his plea will fall on deaf ears. A substitute, then: let his wife be posted off in disguise, to seek of the prophet a hint about the future of his line.

Will the child live? A grievous question.

"Future of his line" and "Will the child live?" Two considerations melded by selfishness into one, in consonance in this dingy, devious character.

~

Meantime, back in Jerusalem, the temple god knows all and waxes wroth. His adversary in search of a future? He shall have it speedily, future and present, awesomely one. He shall have it, poisonous, a bitter cup, overflowing, and he shall be forced to quaff it.

In the episode, the god takes on the abstract quality of fate, an Olympian unconcerned with innocence or guilt, except in one or two matters touching his honor.

The god moves quickly, a blur of activity. His prophet is instructed: Let the message to the woman be dire. (It calls to mind a like message to David from the prophet Nathan after the murder of David's rival, Uriah [2 Sam. 12:15-19]).

Here the word to the mother is, Take it or leave it, mourn, plead as you will — the child is doomed. In this death, the line of Jeroboam is extinguished.

~

That David! He lives in the memory of the god like an icon in a splendid shrine, alight, incomparable. No one like unto "my servant David," who "observed my commandments," who "followed me with all his heart."

The mirror image again. Does not this Yahweh and his illogical fondness for "my servant David" much resemble the David who, it is asserted again and again, follows close the will of the god?

David — lavish, foolish in bestowing his affections at home, just as foolishly vindictive abroad; like the god.

The eye of the god rests fondly on David; the eye of David rests fondly on Absalom. To press the analogy: these pothering parental spirits, yielding and servile, murderous and vengeful, their affections fitful, each helpless to contain the impulses of grim progeny.

~

Jeroboam is determined to rise and shine at whatever cost to others. He has proven intractable, his behavior loathsome, Still, we ask, is mercy a lost cause? Could this be hoped for: If the little son were granted life and health, might the father not undergo a change of heart?

And what of that mother who sets out in a merciless time in search of mercy, hoping against hope — and for her pains is scorched by winds of deific fury? Are her tears worthless?

Like so many of her biblical sisters, she walks the page, nameless, veiled, instrumental to male players, divine or human. She is talked down to, held under tutelage like a child.

And what a brute for a spouse! In effect, "Disguise yourself, say such and such, win for me information necessary to my plans. . . ."

She arrives; the prophet issues judgment. The child must die.

She and her grief are given no shrift. She must hear the worst, and live.

She is put to the door. The awful word a hundredweight in her heart, she returns home. To face the outcome: the death of her child. Yet as far as can be known, she had no more part in the machinations of Jeroboam than did her little son. No matter. The one must die and the other mourn.

~

Need it be noted — we are far short of the Yahweh of the prophets, their clear ethic and inspiration, the God of merciless mercy, impassioned on behalf of the needy and victimized.

With that One, the great seers will commune and fret and contend — and now and again wrest from the deity a change of heart.

Nothing as yet of this holy conflict, of the God of yielding heart. We are on a savage terrain, more akin to the landscape of a Homer or a Sophocles or an Aeschylus. The god is aroused. Someone has exceeded the human measure, overstepped a taboo. Someone (and not necessarily the transgressor) must pay.

Who shall pay and pay? The innocent, the inarticulate. Women, children, infants even — on these the lightning falls. Thus the great ones contrive a god apt to their base instincts. And on the "deity of choice" they confer a habitation and a name.

Of compassion? In heaven as on earth, the quality is in short supply, a veritable seven-year drought.

14:6-20

Neither party to the present imbroglio, the deity or upstart Jeroboam, will concede a point. The adversaries dig in. Hearts grow hard. And nothing of merit or moral improvement follows; literally nothing. The child dies. Point one for the god.

And the father? He dies, as far as is known, unconverted in behavior. Point two for the god?

14:21-24

Our attention shifts to Judah and Jerusalem and King Rehoboam. His father Solomon died a generation before. Since then, Judah and Israel have been locked in conflict, a veritable Thirty Years' War.

Talk about decline yielding to catastrophe. In one generation, psychology, symbol, event — all fell to disarray. The old gods, evicted by David, crept back under Solomon. Now the images are everywhere, cloning their kind: steles, shrines, ritual prostitutes. And all the while the king preserves the temple show, with official pieties and placations.

14:25-28

The generation has regressed from a golden age to a bronze, literally and figuratively. Treasures of temple and palace, including the golden shields borne by the king's guard of honor, are seized by a foreign potentate, the pharaoh. The king, with far less resources to hand, must fashion new shields. He does so. They are of base metal.

And so, by implication, is he.

A Line of Nonentities (Chs. 15–16)

15:1-24

Decline and fall. King follows king, a line of nonentities, royal puppets. Little of note to report. And the style of narrative befits the events: each ruler is disposed of with a tone of disdain, mercifully brief.

For instance. A certain Abijam rules in Jerusalem — a short, unsweet reign, to be sure. His name is culled from nameless deed — in sad contrast to the shining memory of ancestor David.

In the deific mind a distinction grows apace. The memory of David towers, peerless. A colossal hero, a myth. For David's sake the temple god allows the kingly line, by now undistinguished if not nasally offensive, to perdure. The incumbents stagger along, like topers who cannot walk straight, but can run. Crookedly, can run to ruin.

~

We are offered a relief of sorts in the person of a king Asa. This one is granted a long life, ostensibly to clean up the act of his forebears. He sets to with a vengeance, we are told; burn, topple, out with the prostitutes, down with the idols.

Alas, not every "horror" is expunged. And the wars continue, a bloody bore. Boring to the author as well, who would have us yawn along with him, as he repeats the interminable phrase: "King [So and So] of Judah and King [So and So] of Israel were constantly at war with one another, as long as they were in power."

And one thinks: With internal hostilities mindlessly erupting and apparently beyond resolving, what need of enemies at the gate?

15:25-34—16:1-7

The unfetching ways of the world are in full play. Alliances are forged, then dissolve in a mist of blood. Enemies become friends and friends former friends, swords at the ready. Fevers and chills, chills and fevers. Former allies declare war, then re-align. Subordinates turn traitor, destroy their royal patron, and usurp the throne. Some kings live into old age, a few virtuously, most viciously. A number are summarily assassinated.

16:8-22

We come to a tale of effrontery and betrayal. In and out it takes us, round and about, a circumnavigation of mindless mayhem.

A foul act dramatizes the ideology of a noisome, tainted line. One incumbent, a certain Zimri, "committed treason and killed the king." He reigned, under siege, for seven days. Then he entered his palace and set it afire "over himself." Thus, as he madly judges, settling scores with his tormentors. Though perhaps not entirely to his own advantage.

~

Now and again, as in the story of Jeroboam, an entire family is exterminated. Then the avengers themselves fall to the blade of an enemy. And all such horrors, it would seem, are in close accord with the will of the god of Jerusalem, a personage long of memory and given to spasms of reprisal, as apt to take up arms against rival icons and claimants, as against those who create and venerate such. And opaquely, is often displeased with those who destroy the makers of idols.

~

The kingdom of Israel is a broken pot, its shards beyond repair. Contradictions yield to gravity's pull. Like a weakened wall the kingdom wavers, then falls. Falls northward, falls southward. Israel divides in two.

16:29-33

In the tally of royal delinquents, one, Ahab, shines for innovative, spoliating wickedness.

He takes a foreign woman, Jezebel, for wife; of her, more will be heard, though little of good. Shortly after the forbidden nuptials, the king goes over publicly to Baal, builds a temple to the god, and on occasion prostrates himself before the image.

16:34

A dying fall, to be sure.

And as to evil, there is yet worse to report. A certain Hiel rebuilds the town of Jericho. In the course of setting the foundations, he sacrifices to the gods his firstborn son. And in fortifying the gates, he slays his youngest son.

Thus, to the sound of shofar and war drum, the dizzy dance of empire spirals down and down. To the void.

At Long Last, Relief: Elijah the Plainspoken (Chs. 17–18)

We have noted the phenomenon before. When the god deigns to mingle with the great ones of this world, his temperament grows highly suggestible. He takes to himself the ways and wiles of kings — and not always to his own improvement.

Indeed, in his worldly sojourns the deity comes to resemble their earthly majesties. His moods darken; he grows crusty and petulant, inclined to favoritism, jealousy, and vindictiveness.

$\sim$

And when the deity dwells among prophets and saints, those ardent, valiant truth tellers, the opposite occurs. The divine ethic improves noticeably. The god takes new thought and heart, becomes susceptible to goodness — matches, in sum, their conduct with his own.

Chapter 17

With what relief, then, we leave for a time the murk and storm swirling about the enthroned and their acolytes.

It is as though, after an endless night, the longing of the saints summoned a dawn light. And we are blessed, encountering for the first time Elijah, grand and grandfatherly.

How lovable, this avatar. A simple soul, a prophet malgré lui, all decked out in misadventures and mishaps, in miracles and moieties of same.

When the story opens, the era is a bedlam. King Ahab has gone over to Baal. Elijah knows it, and speaks up. His message is curt: royal dereliction has brought punishment, a long drought.

The word once delivered (and no response recorded), Elijah retires to a wilderness watered by a torrent. It is a time of severe testing for the hero. He will survive, but barely. He will drink from the wild waters; ravens will bear him food.

~

The drought seems endless; the torrent fails. And Elijah is posted away once more, this time to a widow of Zarephath, south of Sidon.

He approaches her, begging a cup of water and a morsel of bread. But she, alas, must deny him; there remains nothing of the kind in her house, "only a little oil and flour."

He counters reassuringly. Let her not grow discouraged; God has promised plentiful oil and flour. And the promise widens: upon the earth a bountiful rain will come.

Thereupon widow, son, and prophet together sit at table. And lo, a miracle! Before their eyes the simple menu grows, ample for their needs.

The god, it appears, has grown merciful. He deals gently with widows and their sons — and with prophets who wander the land, leaning on the everlasting arms.

~

Shortly thereafter, tragedy descends on the household. The widow's little son falls ill and dies.

The mother, distraught, forgetful of the "permanent miracle" of the flour and oil, reproaches Elijah bitterly. Has not his presence in her house wrought this loss?

He answers nothing; indeed, what could he say? Her plaint is illogical, a wild outpouring of grief. Leave it at that. He enters the room of death, takes up the little corpse, and places it on his own bed. Then he stretches over the body three times. And the child is raised.

From utter grief to joy uncontained, a sway of mood. Memories all but obliterated surge back; the mother recalls former blessings wrought by the holy man. She cries out, attesting to her faith in the prophet's high mission.

~

Raising the dead — who has heard the like? And what do we Christians make of stories concerning like powers of Jesus? Lazarus, most famous of the revenants, is summoned from the tomb. Likewise the son of the widow of Nain. And the little daughter of Jairus.

And as though these were a prelude to a greater wonder, the miracle worker himself rises from death, speaks with his own, sits with them at table, accompanies them on the road. He has become "the firstborn of many." Ourselves.

And what do we make of that, we who celebrate each year this conquest of the "last enemy," denying a last word to the empery of death?

$\sim$

Women came to mummy You; trees
on that road, stood in commencing flesh
and said with a new tongue, "I am risen."

A hundred resurrections lined the dawn
but they thought: we will give his ghost cold comfort
and wind him like a pharaoh in long linen.

They had nothing to offer life. Of what use in that mouth
honeycomb or fish? He must grow his own flesh
a tree from its root.

They stand where He cast the squared stone aside.
They run and run, the news
runs, far as the tremendous drowning
world of trees that drank from his infinite
roots;

runs far ahead, far as years,
as morning, as this unhurried tree.

D.B.

$\sim$

A counter, so to speak, to the counter. What is one to make of this millennium and its culture of death, multiplying metaphors and methods of death? What to make of the violence, legitimate, tried and true; the settling of scores, real and presumed? What to make of death rows and abortion mills and smart bombs — each attaching a vile tag to lives deemed "expendable"?

~

The prophet has a word for us, and an act — and an implication of both word and act. Yahweh breathes on the prophet the breath of life, that he may breathe life into a corpse. And we are witnesses of a god transformed, this former enabler of wars and warriors, this guarantor of the victory of death.

Behold this champion of the endangered living. In Elijah, in the mother and the child restored, we are offered a welcome glimpse of "God, giver of life."

~

Chapter 18

Our Elijah is disconcerting. He knows little or nothing of cosmic arrangements we take for granted, of gravity's free fall and little by little, distance and nearness, what is hither and what yon. He is skilled in semi-incorporeal comings and goings, epiphanies and vanishings.

In these proclivities, we note, he resembles other, later prophets (and Jesus too, on occasion).

Now and again, we are told, the king seeks Elijah out — whether approvingly or not is unclear. One matter, however, is clear indeed. Kings are inclined to volatile moods. Royal Ahab, for example, is a regent often displeased with such as Elijah, apt as the prophet is to impede, even to scuttle the king's vessel and voyage.

Now and again, such as Elijah are well-advised to make themselves scarce.

~

On one occasion, the prophet obeys the royal summons. He arrives, announcing his presence first to the master of the palace — prudently, it would seem, in view of a chill in the air. He instructs the official: Announce that Elijah is, for the moment, visible, and in a limited sense, available.

The king enters. His welcome is decidedly frigid: "So it's you, the scourge of Israel!"

Not at all set back, the prophet retorts, "Not I; you are the scourge of Israel!"

And he proceeds to upbraid the king unmercifully for his defection to Baal, and to propose a test, a public showdown between himself and the entire coterie of practicing Baalian priestdom.

Bracing, we say — and bravo! At long last we encounter a spirit undaunted by royal persiflage, threats, blandishments.

～

The challenge is speedily taken up; crowds assemble. A buzz! Which sacrifice, the one offered Yahweh or the one offered Baal, will be dramatically accepted?

The preparations are underway. They prove hilariously excessive, a delight. Entire carcasses of oxen are placed on rival altars. The Baalites, 450 strong, commence a dervish dance, morning to noon to evening, in frenzied invocation of their god. They gash themselves with swords and spears, bellowing all the while, "O Baal, answer us!"

Answer? From the empyrean there arises "not a sound, not a voice, no one listening."

Now, the turn of Elijah. He beckons the multitude: Come near! Then he takes in hand twelve stones, "and repairs the altar of Yahweh, which had been destroyed" in favor of Baal.

Clearly we are at a point of crisis; Moses had taken a like action, ratifying before the people the covenant (Exod. 24:4).

Here, now for a show of power. Elijah drenches the altar with water, not once, but three times — and this in a time of drought.

Is water scarce? No matter; altar and victim must be unmistakably incombustible by mortal fires. He prays briefly and to the point, speaking to the condition of the people, hovering as they are between this deity and that: "Answer me, that this people may know that you are God — and have brought them to their senses!"

Indeed. His plea is answered on the instant, more consummately perhaps than sought: "The fire of the LORD came down, and consumed the holocaust, the wood, stones and dust."

And the people? They stood there, shaking, convinced at last: "!!!The Lord is God!!!"

18:40   A bloody tit for tat follows the triumph. Queen Jezebel had dared slaughter the prophets of Yahweh. Now Eljah rounds up the priests of Baal. Shortly the scene is transformed to an abattoir.

The victory turns ugly; we are in the nightmare terrain of the Brothers Grimm. Personally, Elijah slits the priests' throats, all 450.

Of the pyrotechnics of Elijah — what was the effect upon the rival priests? Were they converted? Did they remain stiff of neck? No matter. They went under, every one.

The quality of mercy? We draw a blank. Mercy is foreign to the tale of this wild tribe — as to its untamed god.

～

And what to make of the rambustious circus, the gods in furious contention with the god? Is the story no more than a phantasmagoric orgy, the half-demented contending against the dubiously sane? What has the wild fracas to do with faith in true God — or indeed, with sanity itself? Of what moment to ourselves?

～

This thought occurs. The story offers a wild parody of a given culture.

Our own? We do well, in any case, to ponder weird episodes, as dramatized in the text, as verified today.

We and our Baals. The gods of the culture — invoked, stroked, placated. A dementia of death lies heavy on us. Obsession with death: death embedded in law, custom, economy, military, courts, jails, abortion mills, death rows. . . .

Death as an acceptable social method, invariably cloaked in military overtones and metaphors, and these wildly and publicly approved.

Thus we are rid of enemies, adversaries, delinquents, the aged and "unproductive," the criminalized, the unwanted unborn. And lately, of "terrorists" and the regions that protect them. Decreeing the "end of states," a useful, chilling abstraction masking the murder of civilians, children, women, the aged. Death, a monstrous idol, its eye fixed on the living.

The god invoked, not when other ways have failed — rather, when alternatives are ignored and contemned. As, at present, in America.

~

After a decade of sanctions against Iraq and the death of over a million children, and with Hussein firmly in power, the debate about "modifying" the murderous decree to something termed "smart" sanctions went on:

> Hawkish officials at the Pentagon have argued that even if the modified sanctions passed at the United Nations, they would have little effect in curbing Mr. Hussein, and that the better route was to try to dislodge him from power.
>
> *New York Times*, 30 June 2001

~

Implied in our ongoing predicament is a socialized, functional despair, a loss of nerve, despair of goodness and reciprocity and the skills of give-and-take, plain speech and respectful listening, the search for human ways of organizing our common life in the world.

~

In our story, Elijah takes his stand on the mountain of choice. Faith, the tale proclaims, is a contest, furious and public. Which is to imply that the Baals of the culture must be toppled, their dominion broken, and their priests — the moguls of money, media, politics, the military, each validating the monstrous claim of death — these must be named, exposed, their dominion nullified.

This is the harsh imperative of the wild conflict between Elijah and the Baalites; the fires are lit, the blade drawn against the spirit of death. This a parable for today, if our lives are to regain value and meaning.

~

And the drought. For three years, the people of Elijah starkly endure. The heavens are shut; the sun like a hot millstone grinds the ecology to a dust. Animals, verdure, humans suffer. Many perish.

And the king? He is in the clutch of the Baals, powerless to alleviate the impasse in nature.

Intervention must be free of taint. Someone of merit and innocence must proclaim a neglected truth and act upon it. The drought is an image, a parable of the spiritual estate of the tribe. It is a scorching reminder of the despair that follows on servitude to false gods, those "nothings," those "works of our hands."

The people, from the king and his court to the least of his subjects, are powerless. They have fallen away from the human ideal, are reduced to mere "dwellers on the earth."

Then, relief. There arrives on this sterile scene our freewheeling prophet. His agility, his ecstatic dance, whirling in and out of time, place, and gravity, his nimble act of appear-disappear — these signify a notable inner freedom. Conflict gathers force. He bears an abrupt word of truth, a defy to the king and priesthood, a summons to a showdown. Only after daylong conflict and the death of the priests can the portals of heaven be opened and the rains fall, healing the tormented land. This too is a parable.

~

Relief is slow in coming, tormentingly slow. The prophet too must await the healing rains. Alone, he climbs Mount Carmel. At the summit he falls prone, limp and exhausted. Now at length shall the land, the king, the errant people, and yes, himself — shall all know relief? Relief from the burden of falsehood and fear, the bondage to untruth, the empery of death?

The rain is cruelly delayed. Seven times Elijah must dispatch a servant to discover if perhaps a sign, a cloud, might form in the heavens. Six times the answer is "Nothing."

A final try. And the servant returns, his face alight with a wild surmise: "I saw a cloud no larger than a man's hand, rising from the sea!" (18:44).

Sweet relief at last. Minuscule at the start, the cloud grows great, multiplies, extinguishes the sun. Now the cloud owns the sky, a cavalcade, sovereign, overflowing. And the rains beat down.

Elijah and Elisha: God's Chosen Chooses (Ch. 19)

King Ahab meantime returns to the palace, to recount the events of the day to his waiting spouse. Jezebel rises, her brow a midnight. She looms above him, a berserker, a shrieking Clytemnestra. Her priests are slain, her power broken, Baal discredited!

A message then to the besotted prophet, that crippler of her designs. Let him know, she has sworn an oath. Untroubled by scruple, her powers terrible, the redoubtable queen mounts a plenary retribution. By the morrow, Elias will join in death those he has slain.

The message arrives like a wildfire. Elijah recoils in fear and trembling. At all costs he must escape this retributive Erinys!

~

Alas, in the crisis his powers of dislocation fail. If he is to survive, it must be by way of a harsh journey. Wearily he undertakes it, a day's trek into the desert. At length he comes on a great broom tree; in its shade he falls to the ground, utterly disheartened, and prays for death. Mercifully, slumber overtakes him. And in his sleep, an angel stands at his side. Food and drink are proffered. He must rise and eat; the journey has hardly begun: ". . . in the strength of that food he walked forty days and forty nights, to the mount of God, Horeb."

~

The wicked queen of the north has precipitated the flight. But no evil, only good, has come of her designs. To the prophet the truth of his vocation, access to the wellsprings of prophecy, the work ahead — all these are revealed.

But not in Jerusalem, be it noted. Elsewhere, afar: in a harsh desert sojourn, in reliance on providence, whether in guise of ravens or angels. In a bleak pilgrimage through the wilds, his soul stretched to the uttermost.

Then another Herculean labor. He must ascend the mountain of Moses. Resolve and act! In a harsh, uphill pilgrimage, meaning and direction stand revealed.

~

"To the mount of God, Horeb." What has brought him so far, to this sacred eminence of covenant, the Sinai of Moses? An instinct deep within, a voice beyond words, an emotion welling. A return to sources, lost connections restored.

Under the sign of death, the mad queen's threat, comes this rebirth. And in this place, where an epiphany blazed on Moses, a like event is granted Elijah.

~

First, commotions in nature — hurricane, earthquake, fire.

Then a "tiny whispering sound." To this he must render full attention, be mind-full.

Did he once pray for death? Nothing so easeful is granted him. Only life and its rude burdens, its all but trackless trek. No thunders of approbation, no compassionate, reassuring word — none of these.

Only a whisper, faint as the fall of a leaf. A heavy charge is laid on him, toil and trouble to come, no exemption from spiritual or political responsibility.

Can he dismiss fear? Must he walk with fear? Small matter the difference; he is bidden to return by the road he came. He is to anoint kings, and in due time appoint a prophet who will succeed him.

An epiphany. But no ease, no relief. Something more, something surpassing expectation and effort. As Moses, so Elijah.

~

And when in due time Jesus is transfigured on a mountain, at the center of the Christian epiphany as well — "there appeared with him Moses and Elijah" (Matt. 17:1-8; v. 3).

~

Elijah promptly sets out. He comes upon a certain Elisha, working his oxen in the fields. Elijah — hardly given to preambulations, approaches — disrobes and casts his cloak upon the teamster.

Powerful medicine, unmistakable symbol! The cloak is like a soul close-woven. Cast aloft, it billows out, big as a sky, uncontained. And as it falls in whatever wind, the personality, dignity, even the office of the former owner fall — to another; in this instance, to an unknown.

A death, a rebirth? The cloak resembles a robe for the twice-born. That, or a shroud.

Here it enfolds someone, all unaware, and claims him for its own. To another, the cloak of Elijah; to another — who in turn belongs to it.

And a light dawns. Elisha knows — as he knows the garment enfolding him, or knows his own skin. Or his soul.

And he greatly fears. He is literally cloaked, hemmed in, captive to — vocation. Nothing in life but will be transformed, for good and ill, for suffering and glory. A spasm shakes him. No — or at least not yet! Give me time — let soul catch up with event!

~

And we recall a like scene in our testament, a story of a summons and a "necessary" delay: "Let me go first and bid farewell to my people at home" (Luke 9:61). And Jesus is unsparing: "Whoever puts hand to the plow and keeps looking back is unfit for the realm of God."

~

Elisha: "Let me, I pray, kiss my father and my mother, and then I will follow."

The request is received brusquely. With reluctance Elijah accedes; he has never been one to mince words: "Go, but come back. . . ."

Of the farewells we are told nothing; perhaps the coolness of Elijah toward such niceties shortens the scene.

Something else is lingered over: the destruction of the tools of Elisha's trade. His former trade. On the moment, plowing equipment is put to flames; oxen are slaughtered and their meat roasted.

No possessions. Once the summons falls, even good things are placed in question. They are deemed redundant.

Now for a drama of renunciation. Everything of a former life is gone up in flame and smoke. Free and unencumbered as his mentor, Elisha follows on.

~

How the story touches our hearts, awakening echoes of the first disciples of Jesus, as they leave nets and boats and follow after the rabbi (Matt. 4:18-20).

Also a contrasting story: of the rich landowner who sought to enter the circle of friends. But, but. Jesus informed him of his true moral state (he owed restitution, Jesus declared; he had defrauded the poor). He turned away, saddened; for "he had great possessions" (Mark 10:17-25).

King Ahab and the Deity (Chs. 20–21)

Chapter 20

In our text another war rages, yet another war. Do we require a further example of regression into violence?

The page is before us, our faces pushed deep in the mire and fury of imperialists — Israel and her enemies, one and the same. Awful.

And another side of the royal coin. King Ahab is presented here in a more sympathetic light than Elijah would allow.

The king has survived his terrible wife, a veritable Lady Macbeth. Then a certain Ben-Hadad, king of Aram, appears at the border, huffing and puffing outrageous demands: "Your gold and silver, your wives and children — hand them over!"

Ahab concedes: "As you say, my lord king; I and all I have are yours."

Yet he has the sense to consult with elders. And their courage stiffens his spine. Let the adversary bluster and rattle the sword. The king summons wit to send a mocking reply: "Let not the one who dons armor boast as though he were taking it off!"

So, after all, Ahab and his forces are not to be thought a military pushover. We shall shortly have an absolutely first-rate battle, bloody, no holds barred.

Its import is underscored: Yahweh is consulted. The almighty girds his loins and enters the fray, a strategist and heavenly champion of "his own."

Alas, despite the intervention, all is bleak — the terrain, the numbers. Wonderfully evocative, and fearful too; the chosen are likened to "a couple of small flocks of goats, while the enemy covered the countryside."

No matter. A celestial champion at their side, the Israelites prevail. And we echo the boast of the god: he is like a child-Hercules, triumphant in a celestial nursery. How could the Israelites not prevail — are they not his own?

The popular account is grandiosely sanguinary; the chosen slay "a hundred thousand foot soldiers in a single day"!

~

I can see nothing superior in a man willing to trade his life for public applause, and I can see no more superiority in him when he is a soldier than when he is a prize fighter, a lion tamer or a parachute jumper at a county fair.

The kinds of courage I really admire are not whooped up in war. No one in such times of irrational and animal-like emotions ever praises a man who . . . seeks to restore the national thinking, so called, to a reasonable sanity.

H. L. Mencken

~

Eccolo, Ben-Hadad survives the carnage, and presents himself in sackcloth to Ahab, seeking mercy. He is granted it; "He is my brother" is the response of this surprising king.

The generous gesture of a former enemy prompts a like favor: Ben-Hadad pledges restoration to Israel of towns seized in a prior war. Quid pro quo: a treaty is concluded, and Ben-Hadad walks free.

~

But wait. The two mortals hardly reckon with the god. Hugely incensed! Shall his blood lust be blocked by reconciling mortals? The law dictates another outcome: an enemy is an enemy is _____.

This Ben-Hadad has been delivered over to the "chosen"; how then can he be set free? He must die.

~

We have seen a like celestial behavior in an earlier episode: the condemnation of Saul (1 Kings 13:24ff.) for infraction of a minor rule. And here, unnamed prophets vindicate the loathsome law of blood.

What to say of them — or, for that matter, of their god? Maybe this, sotto voce and in shame: We are granted the gods of our base desires. And they are granted us.

~

In this deity we sense a schizophrenic soul. Shall there be mercy among humans, or shall there be no mercy? Shall the god counsel mercy; shall he counsel no mercy?

We are in the moral penumbra of ancestry: night, and no hint of dawn. Time is a dire "meantime," ominous beyond telling. And divine attributes cannot but reflect the spirit of the times.

If now and again a merciful regent calls a halt to the law of talion, his edict will be denied in practice.

Poor King Ahab. His "default" is declared, and he recedes to the shadows, "somber and angry."

Chapter 21

An episode recalls the punishment of David for his ruse against the life of Uriah. A hint here also of the incitement against her lord of wicked Jezebel. And one is led to wonder: Is her domination a code? Does it hint at cultural fear of strong women? Does Yahweh himself fear this portent?

The king has returned home. What follows is a hilariously vivid domestic sitcom. Ahab nurses a pout. He lusts after a certain vineyard owned by a neighbor, Naboth. The king has tried various devices, proposed purchase or exchange. No luck, no wresting the property from its owner.

So the imperial infant, inconsolable, takes to his bed, turns face to the wall, and refuses all nourishment. Jezebel, perennially short of simpatico, is summoned and stands at bedside. Her contempt is palpable: she chides her recusant spouse: "A fine ruler you are over Israel! Get up and eat; and be of good heart; I will hand you the vineyard."

Resolute, she sets to writing a series of letters, addressing tribal elders and notable folk, neighbors of the vineyard owner. She signs the king's name and affixes the royal seal: There! Her instruction is brutally simple. Naboth is to be cornered and disposed of: "Call an assembly, suborn a pair of scoundrels to stand close to Naboth, accuse him of cursing God and the king. Then take him out and stone him."

Her ruse succeeds. Presto! Recalcitrant Naboth is no more. Then to her spouse, triumphantly: "Rise up, seize the vineyard; it is yours."

Ahab takes possession.

~

But Yahweh is hardly pleased. Elijah the Plainspoken is sent to face off the king: "You are a murderer and more: a usurper."

Ahab can only mutter: "Then you have found me out, O mine enemy!"

The punishment is announced; it is terrible, and includes Jezebel as well. She will be slain; his line will be snuffed out.

~

Two details are of interest. First, the displeasure of Yahweh; how unusual, in view of the moral largesse accorded other deviant favorites. And one wonders: Is the deity's anger directed covertly at Jezebel, an upstart and a woman, rather than at Ahab? If the initiative had been his, would thunderbolts rattle the roof?

In any case, the scope of the indictment widens. Worse than the present crime is adduced; over the years Ahab has bowed to idols and multiplied forbidden images; thus "You have provoked my anger, and led Israel into sin."

The king, who under the prodding of his wife has found crime compatible, now finds repentance expedient. He dons the costume of grief and goes about groaning with remorse. And, as in the defaults of Solomon, Yahweh delays punishment until the next generation.

War, and Yet Again War (Ch. 22)

Once more, an episode of that ancient and famously futile skill, war-making. And, as usual, the god of the warring parties is himself party to the conflict.

The occasion? Kings of Judah and Israel have grown restive. Shall not a military expedition be dispatched to recover disputed territory?

~

As the armies muster, we pause to recall the point of this "religious history." Let us call it an effort to discern, under the smoke and mirrors of battle, God's purpose. Which is to say, the dynamic of a deity only foggily self-revealed, heavily burdened by such humans as has pleased him (sic) to populate the planet. Through these, the ecstatics and eccentrics, votaries and hangers-on, kings and commoners, victimizers and victims — what, pray, may God be up to?

Under the layers of language, the disguised motives and glosses, the logic and contradictions, the falsehood presented as truth and vice versa, the moods of thunder and favor — and perhaps, most opaque of all, the self-interest of all concerned, god and humans alike — what is the point, the plan, the entelechy — if indeed there be such?

~

We groan. What can God be up to? There must be a vast, millennial patience at work as the Deity, close disguised or exiled, certainly appalled, views the planetary spectacle: the gods and their votary-warriors, the unassuageable violence, the wars of attrition, the slaughter of innocents.

The patience of God. These notes are set down in a horrific week. It is as though we must hold our breath between a deed of horror and its condign, certain retribution. In New York City in September of 2001, the World Trade towers fell to rubble. Thousands died. In Virginia, the Pentagon was breached.

And within a week, the giant flexed his muscle and struck back in tit-for-tat savagery.

~

And meantime, in our time as well, the monstrous bloodletting named history (yes, named sacred history) is accompanied by incantations of "temple of the Lord, temple of the Lord," "true religion," "divine choice," "my son David," and so on and so on.

Translate, the task.

~

God replies:

These people want the kind of prophet who goes around full of lies and deceit and says; "I prophesy that wine and liquor will flow for you." (Micah 2:11)

God says:

I hate your religious festivals, I cannot bear them! When you bring Me burnt offerings and grains offerings, I will not acept them; I will not accept the animals you have fattened. . . .

　　Stop your noisy songs; I do not want to listen to your harps.

　　Instead, let justice flow like a stream, and rightcousness like a river that never goes dry. (Amos 5:21-24)

~

We return with a sigh to the god and his wars.

The deity is consulted on a weighty matter. And of what advantage, we wonder, this access to the god? What measure of truth might be presumed when the "ecstatic" mediators are actually in employ of the king? Are they not indebted? Do they not owe their patron a response favorable to his designs?

And what would befall them if their intercession balked at his designs? Would they suffer replacement, or perhaps worse?

In any case, the kings seek counsel with regard to the war. And into their presence arrives an entire school of palace prattlers, four hundred strong, babbling like a rabble.

This: The god says, Right on!

But. Suppppose they had reported this: The god says, No way. Disaster lies ahead!

In that hypothesis (or its opposite, the present report, for that matter), what "religious" knowledge is gained regarding true God, the God of the prophets, or of Jesus?

No matter the outcome of the consultation (yea or nay as to proceeding with the campaign), this might be ventured: We have learned little or nothing concerning true God.

Which is to say, the voice of the god is heard in time and in this world. The world of the Fall. The deity is a military strategist; in this, he wonderfully resembles his mortal clones, the school of babblers. Like them, the god is in service to the royal court.

~

The scene proceeds. Fervently, the pseudo-prophets approve the military campaign.

But King Jehoshaphat of Judah remains uneasy. These, after all, are not his own prophets; they are Israelites imported for the occasion. He seeks another opinion. Is there not a prophet whose view of the venture might be thought to differ?

There exists such a one; a certain Micaiah. For good reason, and by consensus of both parties, he is absent from the scene. The king for his part hates him fervently, and so confesses, "He prophesies not good, but evil about me."

And our ears tingle. Can it be that at the edge of this absurd scene of bloodthirst and chicanery, there stands a vessel of truth? One who has been pushed out of the assemblies of the Kingdom of Necessity, banished — but also, as one hopes, is absent by choice, in contempt? Does such a one exist?

If so, he will save the day.

He will save this episode as well from the domination of its profitless characters. From the arrogant assumption that no contrary voices exist, that the king and his clones rule the earth unimpeded, that they speak for all. That our humanity owns no better than they.

Micaiah, it may be, will rescue the lorn child of our souls, hope.

Hope on. He is summoned, indispensable Micaiah.

~

22:13-28

The prophet is shortly under duress.

In a quite wonderful literary aside, the messenger, a sycophant with an eye to regal interests, sotto voce offers Micaiah advice. Let him be sensible, alert to the main chance. Join with the majority: "The prophets are as one in speaking of a favorable outcome. Then agree with them!"

Micaiah agrees only to speak what the Lord says to him.

The two enter. The scene is formidable: official faces are set in a mineral solidarity; a full and formal court is assembled — would-be prophets, diplomats, hangers-on, even a visiting king. Then the babblers, blessing the king's futile exercise.

At first Micaiah joins them: "Go ahead, you will succeed!"

His body language and the tone of his voice are rife with mockery.

At the sight of him, the king is exasperated. In such an assembly he must measure up, vindicate himself: "How many times must I adjure you, tell me only what the god ordains!"

Micaiah, in ecstasy, ululates poetically:

I see
Israel

scattered
over the mountains,
far away —

a flock
and no
shepherd.

No one
to guide,
to lead —
baa baa,

black sheep,
white —

let every one scatter
homeward —
or

to
no
home!

Exasperating, consummate irony! Micah rubs the truth like an abrasive against the king's ego:

This
I saw:

The Spirit
said
to the god,

"I
will deceive
the king."

And
the god
asked, "How?"

And the
Spirit:

"I
will become

a spirit
of untruth

and enter
the mouths

of all
his prophets."

And
the god
said:

"Deceive him, then.

"Go,
do it."

~

The passage is properly prophetic; and to that degree, out of place and time.

And yet, and yet, how we seize on it. The words are mysterious, subversive, dislocating — and to that degree, reassuring.

Through such images and dramas, ironies, and twists and turns of purpose, we are invited to ponder. According to Micaiah, God has assembled the heavenly court, as in scenes described by the prophets and our book of Revelation.

Then and there, the prophetic "spirit" is personified and summoned forward; but with a crucial flick of a whip.

An omniscient observer conveys a wonderful irony. The spirit of truth invoked by Micaiah will indeed testify on earth — but in utter opposition to the king's design: by becoming a "lying spirit."

~

The spirit is sent forth with a strange task: to settle like a wasp on the lips of the court prophets. To sting them, to inject, infect them — with untruth: "You will entice, and you will prevail. Go and do it!"

So the charade proceeds, the babbling of quick victory and deliverance.

Thus we have it: a sophisticated peeling away of layer upon layer of pretension and folly. Worldly, foregone, smug conclusions are split down the middle like a rotted arras.

A canny trickster, the holy enters a blasphemous scene and kicks over the game table.

~

Too much to be borne, this Micaiah and his ululations! The chief bab-
bler comes forard and strikes the prophet. The king validates the insult
with a punishment. "Until I return safe and sound," Micaiah is jailed and
issued the scantiest rations.

And Micaiah, in no wise put down, retorts, "If ever you return safe
and sound, it is because the god has not spoken through me!"

Wonderful, unflappable courage. We shall see it again and again in
the prophets: a word of truth in a place (usually a palace) consecrated to
untruth.

The saving word is followed by swift punishment. And altogether in-
effectual: no throttling the truth teller.

~

And what of ourselves? Blessed or cursed, or both, immersed in the
sterile terrain of the kings, we seek the truth of God, God's hope, an ethic
worthy of the God of love. The search goes on. Through a torrid "via
negativa," the human caravan drags along through a wilderness, centuries long. Exiles as we are, morally distempered, we confess: Along the
way we fall, time and again, to crime and default.

And our fate? It remains uncertain. Smoke and mirrors. The dark
gods shadow us, those awful images borne along in the caravan. They
whisper seductively, urging us aside from the true way into an abyss of
confusion and despair.

~

In the federal courtroom in Portland, Maine, six Christians were on
trial in the summer of 1997. Their crime: they boarded a "nuclear capable"
destroyer of the U.S. Navy, poured their blood about, and worked sym-
bolic damage with household hammers. Thus to enact the words of Isaiah (2:4): "They shall beat their swords into plowshares and their spears
into pruning hooks."

~

What followed is an old fiction, a mick-mock trial. In short order the defendants were criminalized. Testimony relative to intent, to international law, to the "necessity defense" or their religious convictions was judged irrelevant, and forbidden.

The charade was breathtakingly banal. The jury was instructed forcibly: Honor the law of the land. The only question before you is this: Did or did not the defendants perform the acts adduced? (Which acts, of course, they freely admitted.)

They were shortly declared guilty, and thereafter sentenced to prison.

~

In our story of the prophet before the king, we stand at an oasis of sorts; it is dry as bleached bones. A cry goes up: Punish the truth teller!

And we pause. The futility, the idolatry implicit in the cynical proceedings, the god-to-be-consulted, war in the offing, the kings and their stroked egos, the noxious school of sycophants.

An alternative — the king seeks an alternative voice! But does he? A courageous one stands before him, offering an alternative.

Silence him, strike him, jail him!

No ethic prevails on the polluted air; the sole question is, Who shall be winner, who loser?

No ethic, until the prophet speaks. Then, all ironic, an ethic emerges from the big lie, pushed hard. Utter nonsense is that babble of "you shall prevail."

~

This is the hardest thing of all: to declare the absence of God, and in an utter vacuum, the overweening presence of the god, the idol, the lie. The nothing with a name.

And another noxious presence as well: those who testify to the lie, stand by the lie — and so bring about the trial and punishment of naysayer Micaiah.

His crime? Rare, rare in these pages! He vindicates the truth of God. He names, mimes, unmasks the gods and their kept votaries, declaring their untruth null and void.

The God of Micaiah stands with God's own, laved in contempt, marked for punishment. And nothing will ever be the same.

Shall Micaiah grant them validity, these king-killers? Shall he weigh their military "chances"? Nothing of this is his affair or skill or inclination. Nothing of this highfalutin nonsense.

Exorcism, eviction — these are to his purpose. And irony, and holy duplicity. Let the spirit of truth become a "lying spirit." Thus the lie, insisted on straight-faced, repeated, incanted — on the moment is delegitimated, unmasked. Undone.

In sum, catch the conscience of the king! Act "as though." Compose a supreme fiction, a drama. Let it be as though you accepted everything — human life, death, history itself and its purported makers and breakers — on the terms of the killers themselves.

Act "as though." As though God, all said, has no terms, no other version of the human than theirs — dog eat dog, kill or be killed.

Then spring the trap.

And you, Micaiah — pay up.

~

The scene is like an archeological dig: what stands revealed is both horrid and glorious. Base humans, a multitude of these. And one human, noble, vindicating.

~

Let us suggest a parallel from our lifetime.

In the mid-eighties, the people of a Guatemalan village were exterminated. A few escaped to tell the awful story.

The war winds down; relatives and friends of the slain take resolve. They must exhume the corpses, pray and weep over the bones, reclaiming the memories and honoring, as best they might, the dead.

What a task!

And ourselves. Deep, deep into the psyche of culture and humanity and the start of things, our pseudo-prophets and their kings, those we have been urged to trust and rely on and obey — deep, deep we must dig. So deep that we uncover a mass ossuary of deception and crime, darkness upon darkness, emptiness upon emptiness. Bones, dry bones. Ourselves, our story.

The map that leads us to the scene of carnage, to the site of the hidden boneyard, is our bible. Dig, dig. Until memory is freed, the bones stand articulated, the animating spirit cries out: Hope! Justice!

Unwanted, despised, put to naught, feared, the bones must be uncovered, rescued, cherished, taken in arms, wept over, brought home. Our own at last.

~

22:29-54

The death of Saul and of Ahab — how horridly alike!

King Ahab rides to battle. He proposes to his crony, Jehoshaphat of Judah, that Jehoshaphat wear his royal robes. He, Ahab, will disguise himself as his companion king.

The enemy is hot in pursuit of Ahab. Jehoshaphat, on the other hand, is not the prey; strangely enough, he is protected by being recognized.

Guises, disguises! Things turn badly for Ahab. By ironic mischance, an arrow brings him down. At sunset, victim of his own violence and deception, he dies; from the floor of the chariot, dogs lap his blood.

A bad ruler made worse by bad luck, this devotee of the Baals, married to a murderous vixen.

And finally, the best-laid plans of this mouse or man go wildly awry. (Surely the anti-hero of Melville's masterpiece is well-named for him.)

~

The succeeding incumbents to the throne are of scant interest. One of them scours the seas for gold, as in the glory days of Solomon. His fleet, alas, is wrecked. Other worthies bow and scrape before the Baals. Little of value comes of the idolatries.

And the people, disoriented and oppressed, count for nothing.

In sum, the kingly line is petering out, a sorry lot. And the prophetic fires are banked — or extinguished.

~

Still, judgment lies on the pages, not to be missed. It is implicit, but to the observant eye it stands, a rubric on the text. Misdeeds and crimes and bogus glory are themselves the judgment, a vivid commentary on the futility of foolish potentates.

Futility, the foolish potentates. Who reproduce, mime the ancestors, perdure in wickedness and war. To our day.

SECOND BOOK OF KINGS

The division into First and Second Kings is unknown to the Hebrew bible. Unifying the book makes more sense. We have a manifestly artificial division here, in midcareer of prophet Elijah and King Ahaziah.

An occasion, perhaps, to pause and formulate a few of the questions the text thrusts at us.

- What message is conveyed in this or that episode? So goes an invariable first query. Or more to the point, perhaps: What light does a given episode shed on the divine hope for our human tribe?
- Through this or that story, how fares God's project for our world — a purpose presupposed as the driving soul of biblical narrative?
- Might this or that incident offer a glimmer of light on events of our lifetime, a glimpse of the Holy as well as the unholy, the spirits of light and darkness contending in the world today? (Answer it now: Yes, vehemently. This "glimpse," it would seem, is granted, though a considerable clan of experts neglects it entirely.)
- What Presence in the text cancels or empowers the empery of death over time and creation? What Power denies — or solidifies — the boast of the powerful and violent? To wit: "By whatever means called for, we shall prevail."
- In the deeds or misdeeds of this or that ruler, is a moral norm vindicated? Is judgment pronounced or implied?
- What light is offered by prophecy, contending against the vagaries and crimes of the kings?
- What images of God prove robust, commonsensical, true to the test

of experience? Which of them is sage, ardent, clairvoyant, the gift of those who "have seen God and lived"?

- And what images are false, distorted, bogus, self-serving, projective, tawdry, violent, spirits of darkness masquerading as messengers of light?

And so on.

Of Kings and Prophets: Light and Darkness Contending

(1:1–6:23)

For we wrestle not against flesh and blood, but against principalities, against powers, against the rulers of the darkness of this world, against spiritual wickedness in high places.

Ephesians 6:12

Ahaziah: Another King Falls (Ch. 1)

In a tone of subversive mockery, the story of King Ahaziah continues. Injured in a free fall from his balcony, he is driven to this: he sets about dispatching messengers to consult with a god, Baalzebub. Shall recovery be granted him?

Thus he invites a further spate of ruin. (One notes that the god thus petitioned is well-known to Christians and Jews, under a number of metaphors and names.)

The name of the deity invoked, Baalzebub, "god of the flies," is a derisory title, a pun on his true title, Baalzebul, "god the prince." (He is mentioned in Matthew 10:25, and in Matthew 12:24 he is called "prince of demons." Quite an eminence.)

~

The temple god is alerted to the king's last-ditch machinations. Elijah is summoned; go intercept the messengers and say this: "Is there no god in Israel, that you should seek after Baalzebub the god?"

The question is ominous, ironic, wonderfully indignant. It contains, like a hidden charge, its own answer. The king is doomed from that hour.

Doomed or not, he determines to take revenge on upstart Elijah. He dispatches a captain and fifty men to seize him.

And what a scene follows, as though painted by a child or a genius, an icon blazing with primary colors. Jagged peaks rise abruptly; at the heights, in solitary majesty, Elijah is seated. The armed pursuers approach below. They call up, demanding that "the man of God" come down.

His response is like the blast of a shofar, fiery with resistance: "If I am a man of God, let fire descend from heaven and devour you, you and your fifty soldiers!"

And whoosh! it is done. Flames erupt; to a man they vanish in thin air. A second band is sent out; the fifty suffer a like disastrous outcome: death by incineration.

The king is a slow learner. And cowardly to boot: on his foolish errands, others perish, his military being woefully expendable. His motto seems to be: If a given tactic fails, repeat it, enlarge it.

More is better; let a third force be dispatched.

But this captain, appointed to head the doomed (and himself perish), is no gull. Both judicious and pious, he takes counsel with himself: Why must I and mine incend like the others?

How roles are reversed! He falls to knee at the base of the mountain, and calls up a piteous plea: "Already one hundred men and two captains have perished. Now may my life and that of my men have value in your sight!"

An angel counsels the prophet: Go down; do not fear. Elijah does so, and is led before the king. No whit daunted, he announces again the punishment appointed: death of his highness.

~

The destruction of the soldiers, we are told, is unprecedented in the annals of Elijah. One hopes so. In these awful confrontations, death and violence are simply the order of the day: tit for tat.

But what of an alternative, a less lethal way of proceeding? The question, alas, has not arisen.

That "better way" would suggest that if a king misbehave, a prophet or the god of a prophet might seize the occasion, urging a change of heart in the delinquent.

Nothing of this. The law of the universe, as promulgated here, is devilishly simple and brutal — a variant, really, of the law of the jungle. Action equals (and demands) reaction. When rulers sin, the god (or gods — it matters little at this point) on the instant launch lightning bolts. The likelihood of a change of heart on either side (and surely change, conversion, is required by humans and gods) — this remains remote in hope, and rare in fact.

Our text illustrates a fixed, essentially sterile moral universe. A moonscape of the soul.

"My Father, My Father, the Chariot of Israel and Its Driver!" (Ch. 2)

But not altogether. We enter the rapture of Elijah into high heaven, and his succession by Elisha.

This Elijah — what relief he offers! No lackey of kings, a hermit soul, speaker of unwelcome truths, fierce slayer of adversaries. And truly a forerunner as well. His descendant in spirit, John the Baptist, will appear in due time, austere as the great ancestor, clothed likewise in camel's hair and a leather girdle, speaking truths equally unwelcome (Matt. 3:1-13). And for that, paying up, dearly (Matt. 14:1-12).

A notable difference as well marks the two: John foreswears the violence of his antecedent, while keeping the verbal fire intact. And John "runs before" a totally other God than the deity of Kings — the disarmed Jesus.

～

The day of ascension nears. The drama proceeds like a Greek tragedy, all fire and anguish and wonders from on high. Elijah, it is decreed, must embark on his celestial journey alone.

Three times he contrives, trying to separate out from his disciple; three times Elisha refuses to depart from him. And each time, as the two walk side by side, fifty "brother prophets" approach Elisha with a naive, unnerving query: "Do you not know that today, Yahweh will take your master from over your head?"

~

How do they know it? They are only partially enlightened. Today is the day: this much has been revealed, no more. They will be denied sight of the "sweet chariot swinging low."

It is all classic Greek — perhaps thereby, universal. Three times, three stages on the pilgrimage of Elijah and Elisha. Three "schools of prophets, one at each stage," intruding. And thrice, Elisha must put them to silence.

~

Elijah's departure, its time and mode, is none of their affair; they are surrogates for ourselves, humans unskilled in miraculous meanings. More: it is implied that these adolescent prophets-to-be are given to superstitious curiosity.

~

The procession wends its way, on the face of it no more than a carefree, innocent country stroll. Elijah unwillingly takes the lead, the persistent chorus following close. The friends arrive at the banks of the Jordan. There, Elijah unrolls his famous cloak; with it in hand, he strikes the waters. Meekly they divide. He and Elisha walk dry shod to the farther shore.

It is miraculous, a prelude. The moment, whether of birth or of death, nears. A true "passover."

The supernal moment presses; the two linger for a time, apart. Elijah speaks; his question is pregnant with grief. A death, a departure, in any case a rupture: immanent, awesome, never before or since beheld on land or sea:

What then
can I

do
for you,

before
I

am
taken
up?

Elisha, for his part, is grandly aware, and quite dissolved in tears:

Grant
me

double
portion

of
your
spirit.

Elijah:

You ask
a difficult
thing.

But
if you

see me
taken up,

what you seek
will be granted.

If
not,
not.

A primary belief is evident here: the prophetic Spirit cannot be simply transmitted. It is a direct gift of Yahweh, bestowed on this one, denied that one.

Still, a teasing sign is offered. If Elisha "sees" the miracle of the fiery ascension, the spirit will come to rest on him also.

Interesting too: the "brother prophets" are granted no sight or insight of the miraculous event.

But Elisha is granted this — to see the moment of seizure and ecstasy: flaming horses, a fiery chariot, and Elijah taken up.

And the disciple utters a loud cry:

My father,
my father,

the chariot
of Israel

and
its
driver!

"The chariot . . . and its driver!" How mysterious the cry. Are we witnesses of a scene in which, as some suggest, the "chariot and driver of Israel" are assigned a better, higher office than war?

Further, does the heavenly assumption of Elijah, under this sign of chariot and driver, signal a momentous change in high heaven regarding enmities and killing?

Indeed, who is the "driver"? Is it Elijah, or perhaps great Yahweh himself? And has this realization come to the disciple at the exact moment when he is granted the prophetic office?

Question, questions, and how fruitful. Is the sign recognized and accepted? Does the killing stop here?

~

Washington. President Bush declared at the Pentagon this morning that he wanted Osama bin Laden, the prime suspect in last week's terrorist strikes, brought to justice, and he pointedly recalled the frontier posters urging the capture of criminals "dead or alive."

New York Times, 18 September 2001

~

Headline, same day:

WALL STREET REOPENS SIX DAYS AFTER SHUTDOWN

~

In the madly whirling misadventure we name history, one longs for the entrance of humans into a "still point" where life rather than death is in ascendancy, and even warriors grow weightless and are borne aloft. To a new calling, and a better!

We tread softly here. If the cry of "chariot . . . driver" implies a moral advance, as though the chariot ascended, bearing an only hope — nonetheless, the same carriage falls, victim, alas, of common gravity. The tale goes on. With a thump, the chariot of hope strikes ground.

The text is wild; humans advance and regress. At the point of death, Joash will utter the cry of Elisha. But what a difference! Then it will be a war cry. Old recriminations return; they flood the earth, bathing the last breath of the prophet in blood (13:14).

~

This scene must also be accounted a parable of symbols turned sour, of hope wrecked. The wars, the killing continue unabated.

Aghast, we ride our history. The chariot returns, sets loose a torrent of blood. Still, we take hope. The Targum comments on the cry of Eliseus: "The hope of Israel rests far more strongly in the two prophets, than in a chariot designed for war."

So be it, this small sign, alight, weightless in the heavens.

~

A chariot and driver swing high. And we ponder a gift. An infinitely more persuasive and dramatic "Sign" is granted us. The instruction of Jesus concerning violence is abrupt and to the point, couched in commands. "Put up your sword." And "Love your enemies."

Need it be added to our confusion? The teaching is brutally, pointedly ignored. By Christians, to this day and its fray.

~

When Elisha saw his "father" no more, he took hold of his own garment and tore it in two. Then he rescued the cloak of Elijah, "which had
fallen from him."

~

When Baal Shem Tov stood still to pray, the fringes of his prayer
robe trembled; the fringes "had their own life and their own soul."
They could move even when his body did not move, for through
the "holiness of his doing," he had "drawn into them life and soul."

Annie Dillard, *For the Time Being*

~

Again striking the waters, Elisha divided them and rejoined the broth-
erhood. From their dazed look, it is clear that these saw no trace of the fiery
ascension. Still, their nostrils twitch; something mysterious is in the air.
Like children in a nursery chorale, they question one another: "Why does
Elisha return alone? Where might Elijah have gone, or been taken to?"

They are endearing, this chorus of literalist to-fro children. Undoubtedly, they reason, their master has been plucked hence, but only within
the bounds of this world. He has been taken, as, heads spinning, they put
it, to "some mountain or valley."

But that the event is final, a purging of death through resurrection, or
something of both finality and victory — that Elijah has passed from
time and this world — they cannot remotely imagine. Bewildered, they
mill about, stalemated.

Only Elisha witnessed the fiery event, and its ambiguity. And he is
unnervingly mum.

The event, as far as could logically be judged, is simply a disappearance, a vacuum, a shadow where once a man stood. Indeed, a question of
conventional wisdom shadows the minds of these innocents: How else
but through the "narrow door" do humans pass from the world?

~

And what are we ourselves to make of it, that "ascension" of Elijah? A
stupendous "sign" that abides, a coda, a stigma on the soul of an entire
people, a guerdon of things to come? All these, perhaps.

After the event, the fiery chariot never departs our sky — nor does the cry of the disciple die on the air.

And the vatic cloak? It falls and falls, to the yearning arms of disciple after disciple. To our day, and beyond.

The event is to be accounted a pure gift. A gift to Elijah himself, first of all. A death that is not a death. A departure that is also a descent: for the cloak that rises, falls again. Another, then another claims it and drapes it about his or her person, an ancient power conferred anew, a new mode of presence-absence.

∼

Indeed, concerning this momentous passing, language falters, as in a thicket of negatives: a non-death, non-absence. A mystery that refuses coherence within our limits, that lies beyond, that teases from afar and beckons near, that is ours and not ours.

For all his absence, Elijah abides: suspended in history, living, incorrupt, at a distance. And the memory is so near, so dear. Shall we speak of a great and grand life writ large in our text?

And for our sake as well — no outcome? A sign, merging with a later, more stupendous sign, to remind and hearten? A signal to ourselves, all but swamped as we are in a culture of death, that the last word has been denied death — that the undoer of the living has lost its sting?

∼

If Elijah did not die (the text leaves the matter uncertain; and Elisha will not or cannot enlighten us), does it not follow that he will return? Speculation is inevitable. It colors discussion and exegesis down through the centuries.

The uncertainty is embedded in Christian scripture as well. The question is brought before Jesus concerning the identity and fate of John the Baptist. He responds enigmatically:

If you
are prepared
to accept it,

he [John]
is the Elijah,

the one
who was certain

to come. . . .

Matthew 11:14

~

It is as though our storyteller were a kind of beyond-your-ken character, a witness of the event. This is the method: the disciples surrounding the audacious occurrence are shown as incurably curious, delightfully naive.

Let them stand surrogate for all who would nose out the mystery. Let these mini-prophets wear furrowed brows, grow intensely puzzled at the disappearance of their mentor. Let them purpose to "get to the bottom of this!"

Against the objections of Elisha, who is both wise and silent (an unusual duo of qualities, to be sure), they set out like a troop of scouts on a search expedition. Three days and nights they scour the countryside. No Elijah! They return, puzzled and put down.

Their bewildered, hangdog looks, their unspoken questions are met with a laconic nonanswer — very Jewish, very Elijan. The disciple has taken on the master's abrupt ways: "Didn't I tell you not to go?"

~

All biblical stories are true. Some of them even happened.

Anonymous

~

Two miracles follow. One is benign, the other a curse and consequence. And each seems authentic, a sample of the storytelling fraternity of prophets passing it on, passing it on.

In the first, Elisha purifies waters which had fallen to pollution and sterility. He stands at a fountainhead named the "Fountain of Elisha," casts salt on the waters, and prays. "And the waters were healed, even to this day!"

The second tale is far more problematic — shocking, even. The prophet passes through a village, and a band of small boys clots. They set to miming and mocking him: "Baldhead, baldhead!" Was he prematurely bald, or was he tonsured, in the way of many prophets? In any case, the cruel jollity stops here; one does not heap derision on an Elisha — or, if so minded, prepare for a dire outcome.

He wheels about and curses the mini-ruffians. And on the instant, two bears emerge from the wood and tear the mockers to pieces, forty-two of them at a stroke!

In such stories, death and life are in shuddering contention. Faith is a crisis, a drama. A prophet walks our world, stops and lingers in this or that town. In one place he restores waters; in another he slays a vagrant crowd of children. Unutterably cruel? Yes.

This is a marked man, apart, a hermit on the road. He sees, judges, acts. He is a terror to afficionados of the "middle way," whose taste runs to an easy faith, who work no great evil, but whose fires are gone to ash, who lack passion for the good.

All said, much like ourselves.

~

This "school of prophets," we are told, was a species of gyrovagues abroad in the land. They were gifted with mild powers of intuition or intervention, exerted on behalf of daily need. Then an Elijah appears, from God knows where. And suddenly the air is charged with danger. Lightning bolts are hurled; chariots commandeer the sky; a prophet is snatched into the whirlwind. From a disciple a cry is torn. And for relic and sign and only guerdon, a cloak falls and falls.

~

And we, what do we see? We mingle with the chorus, perhaps; we view everything "from a distance." A courteous way of saying: we see little or nothing. A little which amounts to nothing. Our religion is mild, devoid of passion, a cure-all.

Was a great seer taken from us? He cannot have gotten far; we shall form a search party. . . . And O for a guide in the fallen world! We are lost in the thicket of Dante's purgatorio.

Elisha: A Prophet to Love and to Loathe (Chs. 3–4)

Chapter 3

An awful tale is told of yet another war. The story is problematic, and worse. And we protest: Why must the tradition continually wound our eyes with stories of hatred, carnage, guile? Must we be pushed face-first into a mess of wormwood? Is this the sole way to unlearn war?

Disturbing, disheartening: the prophet is complicit. Complicit, deeply. And the god of the prophet must also be charged: complicit. It is as though the very guts of the godhead were being dealt out and out, to be woven in a close, awful web. And we are tangled in the web, torn within, like captive insects.

We are drawn to love and admiration of Elisha — and drawn to loathing him. And each, hatred and love, is appropriate. Each befits his veering behavior — prophet, conflicted, unfinished human.

∼

As the stories attest, he loves life and exerts himself unselfishly in aid of the needy. When beseeched to intervene, he even summons the dead.

And yet, and yet. He can be summoned to complicity in evil.

Nowhere is this dichotomy and denial more apparent than in the scene before us. No command is heard (as others have been commanded) to invoke death. Yet he invokes death. He becomes the creature of a despicable imperial design.

It will be helpful to recall that our text leads us far and apart from true prophecy. We wander in a faint penumbra of the real thing, eons distant from its high noon.

∼

So to our story. Kings, as appears once more, are invariably great schemers and circumventers. So Elisha is approached, as was Elijah, to shed light or bestow sanction on a royal proposal. We note his response — and we take heart. He is haughty, aloof. No sycophant this Elisha, no more than his master.

Still, though reluctant, on occasion he consents. He can be persuaded to stand with the king, to serve and advise. Likewise his god can be persuaded: to consent — to serve and advise. In concert, the two contrive circumstances favorable to "victory." They even enlist ecological wonders to aid the king's wars.

~

One can no more win a war than one can win an earthquake.

Anne Travers

~

The oracle Elisha delivers is dire. Let the campaign proceed; it will be victorious. But the text subverts the "victory." The outcome brings only this — a human and ecological catastrophe: "You shall destroy every fortified city, fell every fruit tree, stop up all the springs, and ruin every fertile field with stones."

It is hardly apparent to the prophet (or to his god — only perhaps to the omniscient author) that "victory in war" is a vile fiction, a moral mirage. It has led, leads, will lead entire generations (and their deities) far from the truth of life, far from the God of life.

~

In the East
The dark wrath of people
Is the wild organ music of a winter storm,
A purple wave of battle,
Leafless stars.

With broken eyebrows and silver arms,
The night beckons to dying soldiers.
Ghosts of those killed moan
In the shade of the autumn ash tree.

A thorny wilderness surrounds the city.
From bloody doorsteps the moon
Hunts terrified women.
Wild wolves have broken through the gates.

Georg Trakl

~

War, this biblical war, any war — is it to be named a worthy celebration of the human? The war here recounted must be laid at the door of a celestial-terrestrial trinity: it is the god's war, the king's war, and the prophet's war. Each claims the conflict for his own; each in his own way wages it. And each, whatever the means adopted, accounts himself innocent of guilt.

The campaign ends (one is tempted to say, every war ends) in somewhat this way: (1) a firstborn child is sacrificed as an offering to Mars the implacable: "When he saw that he was losing the battle, the king of Moab . . . took his first-born, his heir apparent, and offered him as a holocaust. . . ." And (2) the war ends as every war ends: with fury against the victor. Fire is sown in the vein of the future. It smolders away, waiting its inflammatory spark: "The wrath against Israel was so great. . . ."

~

Chapter 4

The contradictions of our Elisha! For the sake of others, life wells up in him, miraculous and flowing free. As in the story of the impoverished widow, her children in bondage to debt and marked for slavery.

The popular appeal of such a tale is evident. According to the prophets, "widows and orphans," vulnerable to winds of mischance, merit merciful interventions. As here. A miracle is wrought. Household oil mysteriously wells up and is sold; children are saved. And the widow, be it noted, is hardly reduced to a passive recipient of bounty. She is assigned a role; she is indispensable to the outcome. Let her approach neighbors, borrow vessels, and begin pouring oil from jar to jar. Shortly all are filled to brim.

It is she who enacts the drama; Elisha keeps to the sidelines. Thus he pays tribute to her dignity. And how pleased we are.

A sequel. As so often occurs among prophets (we shall note the like in the story of Jesus), wandering Elisha is succored, fed, and lodged by a holy woman. A bed, a table, a chair, and a lamp — and on the rooftop of a wealthy home, a tiny space, for him alone. Behold the estate of the prophet, modest and adequate.

And the woman seeks no return for her kindness. So, quite biblically, a return beyond imagining is bestowed on her. Though she and her husband are advanced in years, a son is born.

~

If that were all! No, in their joy, catastrophe lurks. On a day that eclipses the sun of their lives, the child becomes ill. In the space of a few hours, "toward noon," the little one dies in his mother's arms.

Yet her faith, never at a loss, urges a next step. Next step? But the child is dead! Despite all, a next step. Something to be done, and at once. The distraught woman takes up the child's body, carries it to the rooftop, and places it on the bed of the prophet. Thus implying and imploring: Death; and please. . . .

The room is empty, the prophet absent. Absent! She closes the door and goes in search of her husband. Grieving, she says not a word of their loss. Only this, with set face and no tears: "I wish to visit the man of God."

He is bewildered; the time is neither new moon nor sabbath. (It was customary on holy days, we are told, to seek intercession of such as Elisha.)

Without a word she mounts a donkey and sets out. The blessing of the prophet has brought her a child; surely the same power would restore his life.

The faith of this woman! She comes upon Elisha in his hermitage, an eyrie on Mount Carmel. Without prelude, and against all custom, she approaches and clasps his feet. A servant of the prophet strives to push her away. But Elisha intervenes: "Let her be; her soul is filled with anguish. And I know nothing of its cause; Yahweh told me not a word."

At last the mother speaks: "Did I ask my lord for a son? Did I tell you not to deceive me?"

Without responding, Elisha turns to his servant: "Hasten, take along my staff. And when you reach the place of sorrow, place the staff upon the boy."

~

Step by step, closer. But the concession by no means satisfies the mother. She clings to Elisha; he himself must come. Finally he yields and sets out.

Meantime, the servant has entered the house of death. As instructed, he places the staff upon the child's body. Nothing; no sign of life.

Elisha arrives, mounts to the room, closes the door, and prays.

But no — more, more is required; the living must contend close with the principality Death. Elisha stretches out upon the corpse, large frame upon small, mouth against the mouth of the child, eyes upon eyes, hands upon hands. He stretches and strains there. And the corpse warms at his touch. Warms, and still no sign of life. How laborious!

After a while the prophet rises and paces up and down, up and down.

Step by step, how the story holds us suspended between we-know-not and a wild hope! Once more, yet once more he stretches over the boy. And suddenly, a small thunderclap. The child sneezes seven times and opens his eyes. Elisha summons the woman, that "good Shunammite," and leads her to her son.

~

The mother — is she an unnamed Martha of the Hebrew bible, surrogate for women who throughout history served the prophets and martyrs? Women who followed wherever the rabbis went, ministering to their needs, offering hospitality in their homes — "a bed, a table, a chair, and a lamp"?

Women who, when dreadful event required, stood at places of execution, and afterward kept watch at a tomb? And this, when their male counterparts kept prudently at home ("for fear . . ."), behind barred doors? Women who for the most part are nameless, who in many instances are shown scant gratitude?

How incumbent on ourselves to thank them, to keep their memories in honor! O good Shunammite!

~

The stories abound and multiply. With a handful of meal, Elisha turns a poisoned stew harmless. On another occasion he multiplies loaves of bread, and "some is left over."

(This will occur again, at the initiative of a Greater than Elisha [Matt. 14:13-21].)

~

And yet, and yet, second thoughts nag. In our story, we have yet to discover an integrated conscience in the "man of god."

(Nor, for that matter — and a grievous matter indeed — have we discovered an integrated conscience in the god of the "man of god.")

We ponder, and are heartened — for a while. The worker of wonders multiplies bread at need, shows a feeling heart for widows and children, turns poison to sweetness — and caps all by raising the dead. Admirable, awesome. We give thanks.

~

Yet even the brightest sun casts shadows; and we have stood in a shadow that darkened the earth. Which is to say, the worker of wonders is susceptible to royal blandishments; and this, be it noted, without regard to the morality of the deed proposed.

Thus Elisha can be persuaded to bend above the war map of a king, pointing out — always with help of the god — the tactic, guileful and sanguinary, that leads to "victory."

A hint that he and his god dwell in a kind of prenatal stage of conscience?

In any case, aided and abetted, the fictions and follies of kings take flesh. Many innocents die. And contemporary prophets go along. We have seen it before, a staple of that era.

Thus these "men of god" offer a pseudo-divine sanction to imperial obsessions — that a given war, any war, can benefit victor or victim. Or that the king's wars can stand in accord with the will of God.

~

Let us enlarge the issue: it stands at the heart of history, and of the God of history. The siren chant of "Victory!" sounds in the ear of every generation, of every high culture. The obduracy, the omnipresent allure, serve to verify again and again the "darkening of intellect" consequent on the Fall.

Victor, victory, victorious! The incantation must, of necessity and experience, ignore the following tasks:

- Tot up the corpses. A greater number of these "trophies of valor" are scattered about on the losers' side than on the winners'.
- Reckon the cost in money. The indemnity of the losers stands higher; to the victor, it is said, belong the spoils. The losers must pay and pay.
- Account for ecological damage. The lands of the enemy are rendered stonier and more sterile than those of the victor. Stonier, more sterile? If only that were all!

~

Attack a village with an A-10 Warthog bomber, and leave a deep, empty trench.

Attack a village with an A-10 Warthog bomber firing depleted uranium, and leave a poisoned graveyard — the people dead, plants dying or sterile, the earth eternally toxic. . . .

Sanctions (a crime against humanity) and use of depleted uranium (a war crime) have killed two million Iraqis since the [first Gulf] war's end. . . .

Philip Berrigan, from prison, 2001

~

We are well-advised not to deceive ourselves, as though we of the second millennium dwell in a better light than Elisha, or were less divided in conscience.

The event we ponder (the prophet in the war room of the king) is repeated in our era. Many who are accounted prophets are easily inducted, give ear to the blandishments of the war-makers. Many who otherwise show tenderness toward this or that victim are also alert to the beckonings of the king; they lend voice and blessing to war and the planning of war.

~

Let us suppose that a national crisis occurs (as it has, as it does, as it will). One or another "religious leader" is summoned to shed light-from-above on the matter; at least, some such presumption underlies the summons.

The rule holds: religion too must be enlisted.

A Virtuous Duet and a Dubious Spirit (Ch. 5)

Another wonderful story. As often in our biblical narrative, we are well-advised to pay close attention. Here too, the point is subtle; who are named in our tale, and who left nameless?

Here: a girl, anonymous; and two kings, of Aram and Israel, likewise unnamed. The story hinges unexpectedly on the words of a captive girl, an Israelite slave in the land of Aram. The girl remembers — her land, her people, and pointedly, the powers of "a prophet in Samaria." Thus she becomes the pivot of our tale and its unprecedented outcome.

She approaches her mistress, spouse of a powerful commander of the Aramean forces. He is a renowned soldier, we are told. But he suffers from a dread disease: leprosy.

The heart of the slave girl quickens with compassion. And more: with purpose. Her words to her mistress are tentative, hesitant, as befits her status. "If only . . ." she murmurs. Thus a matter of life and death hinges on a slender condition, couched as though it were a favor granted her: "If only my master could go to the prophet who lives in Samaria! He would heal him of his disease!"

Her words, a promise, a last-ditch hope, take wing, rapid, inferred. Now they are bruited about amid the powerful. Such words, even though spoken by a nobody, must be taken seriously. What other recourse remains to the powerful, rendered powerless by harsh circumstance?

Naaman, lord and leper, speeds to his king. The provenance of the "slave girl from the land of Israel" is repeated. Her anonymity is insisted on. For a nobody, one thinks, quite a somebody!

Her words, their promise, are like a jewel passed hand to hand, precious beyond telling. The king of Aram moves the action along. Urgency charges the air. Forthwith the king sends his afflicted champion off, bearing a letter to the king of Israel, commending the quest of his friend.

~

Royal hand to royal hand posts the letter. The king of Israel reads, and grows thoughtful. And in a measure — indignant. This Elisha — who is he? Such a one hardly looms large in the realm. Royal I, ragtag the other.

Does ego impede? The king concludes: his own powers are being called on. Strangely, while the thought is comforting, it is also heavy, distressful. He rends his garments; dark thoughts afflict him. Who is this messenger — and what the purport of the letter he bears? Are these no more than a cover for conspiracy?

Power impedes. Uncertainty tumbles about in the king's mind, inhibiting a lucid decision. A voice sounds in his ears, urgent, maddening: "Only take note; the king of Aram is seeking a quarrel . . . !"

~

Elisha hears of the arrival of the ill man, of the king's mistaking ego and perturbation. Aware of his considerable powers, the prophet stands to the unsteady moment. While the king . . . ?

The prophet, it is inferred, also has his meed of ego! Elisha is piqued. Abrupt, a message to the king: "Send Naaman to me, and he will know there is a prophet in Israel."

Is there an implied rebuke here, something of "so will the king know there is a prophet in Israel"? And perhaps: "so will the king know the difference between his throne and my gifts. . . ."

The king, we note, remains nameless — a skillful literary turn. He might be any king at all, is the implication. His kith know fear, gnawing at royal bones. They also overreach, even as they distrust and denigrate prophets.

Why then grant him a name? The story, all said, belongs not to him but to Elisha.

~

Off goes Naaman once more, to the house of Elisha. He stands at the door, not dismounting from his chariot. He is after all, Naaman, "commander of the army of the king . . . important to his lord and high in his favor."

Nonetheless. The genius of the story is a sharp eye and voice, unsparing. The great man stands at the door. And within, one who also knows his quality, his perquisites of spirit, knows "there is a prophet in Israel."

Two considerable egos, and a clash? Elisha, to put matters shortly, is miffed. This one comes seeking a boon. And he will not so much as step down from his dudgeon and favor me with a bow?

Elisha will not deign to rise and step to the portal of his house. He sends a messenger with an abrupt instruction to the stricken man: "Go bathe in the Jordan seven times."

~

Now in the course of a long journey, Naaman has composed what might be thought an advance scenario of the prospective meeting. Noblesse oblige; undoubtedly the prophet will honor the foreign king's favorite.

It is writ large in his mind; it tumbles out, one imagined event upon another. The prophet will "come out and stand there and call on his god and place his hand on my sores and so deliver me from the leprosy. . . ."

And nothing of this transpires, not a whit. Instead, a bootless instruction — and worse: delivered offhand, secondhand. Dumbfounded, stalled, Naaman questions. He is defeated and ironic: "Have we not rivers at home in which to bathe?" And, furious, he turns away.

~

But finally, under urging of his servants, he yields, goes down to the river and bathes. And is healed: "His flesh became again like that of a little child . . . ."

He returns to give thanks. And more: in a spontaneous welling he utters a profession of faith: "Now I know that there is no God in all the earth, except in Israel."

Now Naaman is vigorous, purposeful. He would transport two mule loads of the hallowed earth of Samaria, to be placed on an altar at home. And he presses on his healer princely gifts.

Elisha refuses. What was freely received is freely given. Reward would clog the flow of the Jordan within, the pure, healing current of his soul.

~

But wait. The sublime gratuity of Elisha, it would seem, is ill-received in his household. Someone, somehow, has heard of his refusal of perquisites. That one is offended, set down.

What a contrast here! A servant, a certain Gehazi, is named. He is governed by greed. And weak as well — save for wickedness, in which he is strong.

⌇

Naaman has departed, rejoicing. Gehazi the servant is on a crooked road. Quick as eye after gold, he speeds off in the wake of the entourage.

Is the prophet pleased to wave all reward aside? Gehazi feels a rush of pious scandal: how foolish, to spurn. . . .

Said, then done. He runs after. On the way he composes a wonderfully altruistic fiction. To wit: visitors have arrived at the house of his master. Elisha has noted their need, and sends his servant in haste to ask an alms.

Naaman, hearing the fiction, is quick to oblige. "Would a talent of silver . . . ?" No, double the amount!

⌇

Gehazi returns, the money concealed. But the prophet, who reads the heart of a king, is hardly deceived by this canny defaulter. Elisha announces a terrible judgment. It falls less due to a greedy transaction than to the crossing of his will and the abuse of his name.

The sentence is a hammer blow. The leprosy of Naaman is to fall on the delinquent, and on his posterity: "Gehazi departed from Elisha, a leper white as snow."

⌇

The episode invites pondering. Taken of itself, it summons an Elisha wonderfully integral, free, a man for others. And another side as well: If crossed, he is brusque, implacable, a Daniel come to judgment.

We witness healing, then a proffer of gifts and a refusal. And we long perhaps that the story ended there: period. We would much prefer an untrammeled image: two personages of virtue, Elisha and Naaman; two ideal modes of conduct, gratitude and altruism.

And a double healing, all said — from physical illness, and from least suspicion of greed. Thus everything would befit, each actor edifying, iconic, integral. And ourselves edified.

~

But, but; not so our story. After the healing by our holy protagonist, we must read of an antagonist and crass double-dealing. And our ideal "Drama of the Virtuous Duet" is marred, all but wrecked. Deplorable, the intrusion of this dubious spirit, Gehazi. He darkens the page and lowers the tone of our story.

~

And of course we have missed the point. The Bible has small interest in the "ideal human" or a "lofty tone" — whatever such abstractions might be taken to mean.

Are we tempted to cleanse the book of its dubious characters, grubbing, irksome, besotted, incurably violent — and now and again relentlessly unmasked?

Too bad for us. How rarely in these pages, as in life itself, there appears a saint, a plain-speaking prophet, a martyr. For the greater part, we must endure (in the historical books, in life itself) the carnivore kings, warriors descending like wolves on the flock, court prophets falling in line, people victimized, passive, put to silence.

The implication is unmistakable: the Bible is interested in — us. In the near infinite variety, the verve, joy, terror, the valiance and yielding, the falling and standing again, the crimes and (now and again) the consequence, the denying and affirming behavior, the life-giving, the death-dealing — ourselves. We, the clan of the Fallen Who Rise Again — and the Rising by a power not our own.

We who lurch about the world, strangers to self-knowledge, seldom robust or consistent, now capable of a strong, virtuous act, again of a despicable falling away.

To the attentive, such images, their variety both woeful and wonderful — these strike home.

~

Facing dread offers a chance to repudiate the idolatry of devout ideas, walking free from an infallible ritual against every risk and every demand of dialogue with human need and desperation.

Thomas Merton

~

Our name too is Naaman. We are lepers in search of a healer. And, if lucky and persistent, we come upon one.

And what of the healer? On occasion his acts stand in appalling contrast. He induces health and illness, both. His ethic is stark and severe — yet, unhesitating, he fans the fires of the king's furies.

~

And now and again, we too are tempted. We take a different role in the story; we become unworthy servants. We push base designs and contrive coverups. Only to see, like original Gehazi, everything snatched from us in a moment.

And we wonder: after a condign sentence is passed against the servant, will he too be healed? Is the condemnation implacable — or may a new mercy intervene?

~

The story, in sum, is accounted the word of God concerning human life — which is to say, it tells of a passionate search for healing, of faith in the breach, faith under fire.

It is a drama which easily yields to tragedy. As recounted, the episode requires not only a virtuous protagonist but another, an opposite force of dark appetite and itchy fingers. Thus only can the story be faithful to life.

Such a parable hardly offers a pablum to comfort fantasies, a placebo to ego.

A Gift of Unexpected Mercy (6:1-23)

According to popular rumor, nature itself is subject to the healing glance and outstretched hands of this "man of God." A small wonder is recounted. When an ax falls into the Jordan, Elisha makes the heavy iron rise to the surface and float like a shed feather. And voila! the tool is recovered.

More serious matters summon a greater gift: clairvoyance. On one occasion, the prophet is surrounded by enemies. And lo, he sees — and helps his fearful servant see — "the mountain filled with horses and fiery chariots surrounding Elisha."

Again, we are treated to a wonderfully humorous estimate of the prophet's forthrightness. An adversary of Elisha addresses his king: "The prophet Elisha can tell the king of Israel the very words you speak in your bedroom!"

~

Bilocation too: in time of battle, Elisha flits hither and yon, much to the dismay and disarray of the "enemy." And rarest of all in this blood-ridden saga, an almost forgotten virtue is brought to the fore. Compassion rests even on the enemy.

~

The part played by the god of Israel in the wars of "the chosen" has often troubled. And once more we are told that god and prophet are yoked in war.

(Perhaps our bible is reminding us that, the second millennium underway, we Christians have yet to let go of (1) a god who takes sides, and (2) a conviction notorious and contradictory: it is ourselves, not the current enemy, with whom the god sides.)

~

6:18-20

The story of this strange war becomes unexpectedly hilarious: Elijah leads the hostile forces on a merry chase. At his prayer they are struck blind. Or perhaps they see, but all awry.

We have a parody of military valor and something known as "military intelligence." Misled by a pied piper, the enemy forces are utterly disoriented. They advance — straight into the heart of Israeli territory, Samaria. And shortly they are rounded up, captive!

~

6:21-22

Then the conclusion. All unexpectedly, the last page is not stained with blood, but aglow with mercy. Sword at the ready, the king questions the prophet: "Shall we slay the captives?"

Answer: "Most certainly we shall not. Give them to eat and drink, and let them go their way."

Famine and Fury: War and Its Shadows

(6:24–17:41)

The war has used up words; they have weakened, they have deteriorated like motor car tires; they have, like millions of other things, been more over-strained and knocked about and voided of happy semblance during the past months than in all the long ages before.

And we are now confronted with a depreciation of all our terms, or otherwise speaking, with a loss of expression through increase of limpness, that may well make us wonder what ghosts will be left to walk.

Henry James, in a letter to a friend
at the start of World War I

The Horrid Banquet of War (Ch. 6)

6:24-30

Samaria is under siege, its people in desperate straits. Perennially a horror, war is underway once more. Pretense and royal rhetoric and the will of Yahweh notwithstanding, women and children and the aged and the unborn are tossed about somewhere between this world and hell, jumbled in a sack of misery and endangerment. War. As ever.

Another image. Under the wide-ranging scythe of death, these innocents fall like wheat among tares, indistinguishable from the fallen warriors.

～

And if, for one reason or another, the innocent cannot be outright disposed of (a matter, all said, of expediency, no scruple impeding), there remains another method, no less terrible.

Starve them. Siege brings an entire population to death. Slow, but sure.

(The same method, we note, is translated in modern times against Cubans and, notoriously and lethally, against Iraquis. War, masked as "sanctions.")

~

There emerges from the siege of Samaria one of the most terrible episodes in the Bible.

The atmosphere within the city is rife with terror and helplessness and the servile despair of those in charge. Seeking relief from the stench and smoke, the king of the assaulted city walks the ramparts, solitary, wrapt apart. And a woman approaches, distraught, crying out: "Help, my lord king!"

~

We note, and are startled; both the king and the woman are unnamed. A king, nameless? The omission is rare in the book named for Kings — as unusual, indeed, as would be the naming of the woman.

Do we have here a hint? Are both king and woman brought low by the jackboot of war — each anonymous, a victim, a statistic in the dark calculus of Mars?

The woman has raised a piteous cry. The king, exasperated and powerless, yells a reply, for all the world like the bellow of a struck bullock: "May God help you not at all! Where is my help to come from — would it be from a rock or a hard place?"

(Literally, "Would I help you at the threshing floor or the wine press?" In extremity, each of the two resources gaping empty, proffering nothing.)

Nonetheless, the king's heart is moved. Dregs of compassion stir within him. Half-unwilling, the words sticking in his throat, he asks her: "What is your trouble?"

As if he did not know her trouble — as if her trouble were not his own.

An awful story pours from her lips. It is a story reminiscent of another, of an event long gone — and with a far different outcome. Early in the reign of Solomon, two women entered the audience hall. One bore in her arms a child's corpse. The other carried a living infant. In contention: which was mother of the living child? They approached the king (1 Kings 3:16-28). They received compassion and an equitable judgment.

~

The despairing king walking the ramparts is, to be sure, no Solomon. And one thinks: Would even that paragon of wisdom come on a way to slip the noose, the siege?

The woman, half-crazed, pours out her tale of woe. A few days previous, a friend, a mother like herself, approached her with a horrifying proposal. This, in sum: Today, starving as we are, we will slay and eat one of our children, starting with yours. And on the morrow we will do likewise with my child.

That day they ate their horrid fill. And on the morrow, the mother approached her friend for resumption of the cannibal feast. But the friend reneged and hid her child. Hence the despair, and the sorry ending.

~

It is wartime; we sup of horrors. Abjectly abnormal events are rendered normal. Somewhere in the world, our world, today as then, a perpetual war against children rages. And in Christian scripture, in a nightmare imagery, an invitation is issued to a horrid banquet. The menu? "The flesh of all, free and slave, small and great" (Rev. 19:18).

Talk about indiscriminate taste, the taste of carnivorous Mars! From the banquet we pass to another "indiscriminate" known as war. From banquet hall to battlefield — an easy transition among the filled guests and the fallen warriors. John the seer, imprisoned on the Devil's Island of Patmos, speaks: "I saw the beast and the kings of earth, and the armies they mustered to do battle with the One who rode the horse" (Rev. 19:19).

~

In our lifetime the rich nations sit to table. Their menu? The children of the poor. In John's Revelation, banquet and battle are mutual metaphors. In the course (sic) of battle for economic domination, more and more children become grist for the Insatiable Great Gut.

For more than a decade of "sanctions," vile feeding on the one hand and forced deprivation on the other, the innocents of Iraq are served up.

∿

In the earlier story (1 Kings 3:16-28), Solomon cut the Gordian knot that bound the mothers in contention and bound the infants in death, actual or prospective.

But that tale of wisdom belonged to a time of peace. Sanity, at least relative sanity, was in the air. King Solomon was not driven to distraction by the suffering of his people; he could mull a matter, even a horrid matter, and render a considered, compassionate, equitable judgment.

But this poor king of Samaria — what is he to do? The siege and its atrocious suffering are driving his people mad. Boundaries are down, taboos meaningless.

∿

Roy Longmore, who was proclaimed a legendary figure by the Australian government last year as one of the nation's last surviving veterans of the World War 1 battle at Gallipoli, died on June 21. He was 107. . . .

His recreational habits were altered by the war. Before, he had hunted rabbits, but he no longer had an appetite for firing at anything alive. He contented himself with aiming at clay targets. . . .

Mr. Longmore once remarked in reflecting on World War 1:

"They're no good, these wars. A lot of lives lost, no good at all. There's got to be another way of fixing up these rows without killing each other."

New York Times, 2 July 2001

∿

Our story of the hapless king and the helpless woman ends; the king rends his garments in despair. The fabric of his realm is raveled; personal and public civility are incinerated on winds of fire. The moral order, that noble "taking for granted" (mothers love children; children flourish in the bosom of love), is scuttled.

~

In the story of Solomon's decision, the king's primary office, that of judging justly, was vindicated. But here, what to say, how mourn? In effect, justice is declared null and void. The king is powerless; he rends his garments. What meed of justice can he hope for (let alone bring to pass) when chaos invades minds and hearts, when the seams of existence are turned out and out, shaken by the demon of war?

Justice ends when war begins. Injustice wins when war is declared.

~

And what of justice remains in the outcome? Justice is dead and buried, a lost cause, a corpse all but nameless; on either side, whether victory is declared or defeat is conceded.

The first injustice, the most terrible of all, is war itself.

War: the quelling of the quest and passion for justice.

Mark it well, this loss. Mark it in the despairing king, pacing the ramparts of his city. The ramparts are shaken. Mars rules; the king is hostage to a greater.

~

The king paces the city walls; the woman confronts him. Despair drives her like a banshee to the side of this distracted man. And what can he do? His cup is full to overflowing; her tale adds a measure of gall.

She? She is beyond relief, even the relief of shame or remorse. Should the king judge and condemn her? What can be done against her, what is to become of her, who has become in her own eyes — a nothing? Nothing left to her, no relief save this: the telling of her atrocious story.

Tell it, then.

Does the king's helplessness match her own? Can he assuage her suffering? He cannot. Still, she must tell. War has wrought this: the woman is plunged into madness; the king is powerless. Speaker and listener are throttled in the fist of Mars. There remains only this — Hear me out, my story!

~

The story has no purpose or benefit beyond itself. (Or does it? It is for us to judge.) This is the purest, most austere form of storytelling, this out-pouring of grief and despair. Life is stripped to the bone, the spirit shamed or quenched. There remains her hallucinatory tale, the speaker and the listener, each pulverized in spirit.

And ourselves, the observers — the believers — what of us?

~

The episode seems to end in stews of despair. The woman is half-mad; the king rends his garments. But wait: matters do not end there.

It must be underscored: the awakening of despair is never the intent of a biblical story — quite the opposite. The story is "for our instruction" — that is, to lead us into the dark underground of hope.

Generations come and go; the woman's wild tale burns on the page, as though self-combusting. For our sake. That we ponder and learn, and take hope — even hope against hope. To this, the tale implies, to this pit of folly and madness, war plunges us humans.

~

It is only
for sake of those
without hope
that hope
is given us.

Walter Benjamin

~

The king's lonely pacing, the woman's threnody — these are as old as time. We linger over the text, as multitudes have lingered before us. That ancient siege laid against a city (siege and city long gone), the distraught king, the two women (where is the second — what has become of her?), the children doomed!

And all the wars of the centuries since, the wars of our awful lifetime, the wars that sear every continent, even as these notes are set down. The multitudes, women and children and warriors, fallen under the blade.

And the rulers of the ancient tale, the would-be winner named, "King Ben-hadad of Aram" named. In the short run, he wins. But the Bible has a long memory. Wait and see.

And the besieged king, short-run loser, unnamed.

In our historian's judgment (surely a stroke of literary genius), the point of naming "winners" is to discredit them, to show the folly that turns victory to dust and ashes. Thus each and all — winner, loser — are presented as indistinguishable clichés. "Someone" wins, "someone" loses — the old, wearying fantasy.

~

Ben-hadad directs the siege, tightens the noose. Mothers are transformed to berserkers. And a nameless ruler walks helpless, under siege, under fire (under bombs, under "sanctions"). . . .

What of the king who has ordered the assault? Suppose his forces take the city? Are they to be accounted "winners"?

Enlarge the question. To any sane mind, has there been, in any war of any age, a "winner" in a civilized, recognizable sense? Which is to pose a further question: Did the victorious, by virtue of their victory, become more sensitive to the sufferings exacted — whether of themselves or of the vanquished?

Or did this occur: In the course of "winning," were the winners further brutalized, hell-bent on yet another war?

And as to an outcome of either side: winners or losers, citizens, soldiers — did these determine never to make war again?

Come now!

~

6:31-33

The siege grinds on, bones for baking bread. And a kind of free-floating anger takes possession of the king. He pauses in his tracks. Someone must be blamed for this disaster! That Elisha — who else? The prophet has counseled a foolish resistance, promising the help of that god of his!

(But is not the god of Elisha the god of the king as well? Were it not

153

more logical that the god himself [sic] be addressed? But why speak of logic — war itself being the supreme illogic?)

Torn between wrath and despair, the king confronts the scapegoat. Who stands there, imperturbably repeating an earlier promise: Tomorrow, aid will arrive.

A Moment's Relief: The Siege Lifted (Ch. 7)

7:1-3

We have seen despair on high, and rancor and unfaith. The king who can do nothing can do this: First, rend his garments. Then presto! create a scapegoat, the last refuge of the despairing.

Rancor and unfaith; and then someone, something different. Elisha, and a calm assertion — of what cannot be, and what must be. Will be. On the morrow, relief.

7:3-20

Our scene shifts abruptly, to a quite wonderful aside. A different cast of characters; no more of the king and the wild woman before him, that duet of pure, raving despair.

No more of these. We stand at a crevice under the city walls. A group of outcasts huddles there. And from these, the lest likely protagonists imaginable, comes a word of hope, the first uttered in our dreadful episode. From despair to hope. A hope so close to despair as to offer, at first glance, nothing of resource or light. And therefore, biblically speaking, a word of hope. The real thing.

Four men sit at the gates of the besieged city. Why are they not bearing arms? Why are they not part of the cacophony of despair? The answer is simple: they are outcasts, doubly so: lepers and Samaritans.

Their talk is pure Beckett. The theme: "What have we to lose?"

~

As the nearest equivalent today of these castaways, one thinks of the homeless, the "mole people" of New York City, dwelling in tunnels, under bridges and overpasses, out of sight, out of mind. Cast out from the achievement-ridden, consuming culture — these, our lepers, our human zeros.

Do political platforms include recognition of their plight? These purported humans are not at issue. They count for nothing. They are a "disappeared people," the American version of "lives of no value."

~

Like characters from Beckett or Brecht or Orwell, the lepers of our story have cast hope aside — a hope that, in their circumstance, was rightly discarded as false, fantastical.

No, they are clear of eye. They acknowledge the truth of their predicament: they are a detritus, cast outside the city — a city, in any case, of the lost. They are useless alike to aggressor and besieged.

Their chances of survival? Slim to zero.

~

The only thing to be regretted without qualification is for one to adapt perfectly to modern society. Then he is indeed beyond hope. Hence we should all be sick in some way. We should all feel near to despair in some sense, because this semi-despair is the normal form taken by hope in a time like ours.

Hope without any sensible or tangible evidence on which to rest. Hope in spite of the sickness that fills us. Hope married to a firm refusal to accept any palliatives or anything that cheats hope by pretending to relieve apparent despair.

And I would add that for you especially, hope must mean acceptance of limitations and imperfections and the deceitfulness of a nature that has been wounded and cheated of love and security; this too we all feel and suffer. Thus we cannot enjoy the luxury of a hope based on our own integrity, our own honesty, our own purity of heart. . . .

Letter of Thomas Merton to
Czeslaw Milosz, 28 February 1959

~

Very well, then, the lepers ruminate, our plight being freely admitted, what is to be done, what choices lie before us? We could enter the city, this or that corner or alley, and die of hunger. Or we could shrug off those who first deserted us and pass over to the enemy. It may be that the enemy would turn friend to such as us and allow us to survive. Or they would not.

One overhears the quartet, their ruminations. These are an existential folk, even prophets of a kind. They make no mention of a god who might care whether they live or die — the god, say, of Elisha or of the king or of the people under siege.

~

Yet, let it be said clearly: the conversation of the lepers is of the essence of religion. In their plight and its bleak acceptance, they dramatize essential themes: life and death. So doing, they breathe free; they enter the drama which many, including many "religious" folk, dread and steer clear of, embracing easy despair.

The four weigh what may befall, totting up their chances. And the speculation is by no means to be taken as a tribute to callous fate: "Why should we sit here until we die?"

Wonderfully, their question conveys nothing of the dead despair of the king or the woman on the ramparts, her hallucinatory raving, his rending of garments. Nothing of this. In effect, they simply say to one another (whereas those others cannot so speak): "Something must be done; let us do it."

Feistily, they undertake a search — what way out?

~

King, woman, lepers — we do well to ponder them. Everyone is nameless, expendable, trapped; it is wartime. And yet, a difference is implied, minuscule but crucial: the lepers resolutely move out of the dead zone named despair. They take a step. In these outcasts, imagination takes hold, alternatives, sound purpose. This is a faith that has forgotten to be "religious."

~

The law kicks them out, cancels them. According to its dictates, they are permitted no loyalties — save to one another, save to such connections as they contrive among themselves. No ties to this world. Lifelines, family affections, friends, spouses, children? None of these. The law has cut them loose.

Cut them free? A terrifying, dangerous freedom.

~

A person who has a dreaded skin disease must wear torn clothes, leave his hair uncombed, cover the lower part of his face, and call out, "Unclean, Unclean!"

He [sic] remains unclean as long as he has the disease, and must live outside the camp, away from others.

Leviticus 13:45-46

~

The four lepers — a lost tribe and its skinny lifeline! They have only one another. Theirs is the courage of those with nothing to lose.

They size up their situation, with an admirable realism: "Come, let us desert to the camp of the Arameans. If they spare us, we live. If they kill us, we die."

So. They rise to a common purpose, venturing from their hiding place into the camp of the enemy — who, all said, is no enemy of theirs.

~

Only to find — wonder beyond belief — no enemy at all, not a one! The tents are deserted, the animals tethered and standing. But of the vast army that laid the siege, not a single soldier.

Well, something here is surely to our advantage. Their eyes light up, these pragmatists with empty bellies. (And, we note, no attempt by the storyteller to "sanctify" them, to elevate them above a gritty last-ditch humanity. Only hunger, ravaging hunger.)

And a miracle — food, food scattered and heaped all about: sacks of grain, wine and meat! Life, that overseer of misery, for once has laid a banquet. Let us eat and drink, and afterward, snatch what loot we may come on — garments, gold. And hide it secure.

~

In haste they eat and eat, starvelings in Eden. Then from tent to tent they hurry, a joyous orgy, gathering the plunder that falls to hand. Amid evidence of panicked flight they hop and shuffle, crabwise, an hour of larceny, wild and sweet.

Then they halt in their tracks. Spontaneously each comes on a better, more reflective mind: "We act unjustly here. Beyond doubt this is a day of good news, yet we keep the news to ourselves! Let us enter the city and tell all."

~

They return. And ever so slowly, as morning dawns, the good news is sown like seeds of an unimaginable sunrise. The people, all but dead and gone in despair, awaken. Revelation, salvation — and this by way of four lepers!

The siege is lifted. Ever so slowly, like the dry bones of Ezekiel's desert, a dazed people knit together their frayed purpose, mend despair.

Hours pass. A multitude pours out of the city and enters the enemy camp, stripping the abandoned tents clean as bone. In the markets, food abounds. Crowds mill about the city gates, feverishly buying and selling.

The road of the retreating army is easily discovered: "The whole route was strewn with garments and other objects that the Arameans had thrown away in their haste."

Something Terrible beyond Telling (Ch. 8)

What the prophet Elisha must endure, what things behold, what events and decisions convey. And now and again, one thinks, terror strikes like lightning, revealing a truth which many years have withheld.

Since the healing of the leper Naaman, the fame of Elisha has grown apace. Once more someone arrives in search of relief — this time a king, no less: Ben-Hadad of Aram. He is ill and posts a messenger, seeking to learn his fate: Shall it be death or recovery of health?

We take close note of the messenger, a certain Hazael. A servant, to be sure, and more: a kind of Uriah Heep — darkling, a would-be usurper. He sidles in and conveys the king's request.

And the prophet equivocates. The sense of his response is: What good at this point to tell the the poor man he is doomed? Tell him, if you wish, that he will recover. The word may bring him a measure of comfort.

A further, furtive sense clings to his words. Something hangs on the air, something terrible beyond telling. Unaccountably, at sight of the messenger, Elisha is lost in a painful trance: "He kept his face expressionless for a long time. Then he wept."

This Hazael who stands before him — it is as though Elisha must gaze into a black hole in space, pure chaos. Evil that beggars words.

~

The future is a poignard in its sheath: Is this a dagger that I see before me, the crimson point of a revelation? Elisha is no Macbeth; this messenger is, and worse.

The dagger is drawn. The blade is inscribed "Hazael." He is aimed at the heart of Israel. Against the innocent and helpless, crimes will multiply under his hands — unspeakable crimes.

Elisha looks him full in eye, a Moses proclaiming a decalogue violated. The prophet cries aloud, the truth. This usurper will "burn [the Israelites'] fortresses, slay their best warriors with the sword, dash their little ones to pieces, rip open their pregnant women."

~

Has our lifetime not seen the black hole, the chaos? We have witnessed the crimes of a Hazael, multiplied many times over.

The indictment of Elisha is like a catalogue of the crimes of the so-called Contras in Nicaragua, the Simosa tribe in Salvador, the armed forces of Guatemala, the Tonton Macoute of Haiti — or the might of the U.S. military unleashed, Vietnam to Kosovo to Afghanistan to Iraq.

And after the attack on New York and the Pentagon in September of 2001 — what, where next? We hold our breath in dread. Poor, ravished Afghanistan, poor children of Iraq.

~

The response of Hazael is appalling — and instructive. Does he grow indignant at the accusations, angrily refute them? Not at all — no hint of denial. He fairly grovels before the prophet: "What is your servant, who is but a dog, that he should do this great thing?"

Thus his summary of the appalling charges, the awful phrase, accepting, pouncing, cringing, evading — "this great thing." His sole theme is a craven self-deprecation.

End of interview. Hazael returns to the king. Duly he delivers the message of Elisha. Then, on the night following, he enters the sickroom and suffocates the king in his bed. Shortly thereafter he claims the throne.

These people — for intrigue, assassination, betrayal — are surely the ancestors of the Medici! Or of _____.

The Blood of Kings — and Queens (Chs. 9–11)

Chapter 9

Another era, another king. This one is to be anointed by a young prophet of the school of Elisha. Under instruction, the youth goes in search of the royal candidate. Uninvited, in no wise daunted, he enters a conference of military leaders. They greet him, an interloper, with contempt. A mocking appellation — "this fool."

The protégé of Elisha shrugs them off. He announces in level tones that he bears a clue: the king-to-be is a military commander. The status is underscored: he will arise from their ranks. And more: he will bring down the house of Ahab — including the insufferable Jezebel.

His words lamentably come true. Murder upon murder, treason, usurpation follow close. To cap the bloody sequence, the king orders Queen Jezebel to be thrown from a high window; her corpse is devoured by dogs.

Chapter 10

Imagination is plunged in a bloodbath drawn by this kingly line of killers and their cohorts. Mayhem rules the page. And we are appalled. The episodes, detailed, sanguinary — are they set down as a kind of expiation of history — a past, presumably accurate as to awful events?

And more: a past which resembles our own times?

(We have raised the question before: Is this storytelling a way of exorcizing, disowning, casting aside once for all the sword of the ancestors?)

~

An earlier oracle announced the extinction of the line of Ahab. Such pronouncements bear a harsh aura, a kind of Greek necessity. They set in stone the will of the god. What must be, shall be.

And more: Whatever blood must be shed, whatever crime committed is redeemed in the act. The one who strikes does so in accord with the divine will; the act symbolizes fealty to the one on high (and a shrug of indifference toward the victim). Thus, as our Bible starkly reminds, a certain brand of religion is enlisted in bloody deeds — even as authentic religious sense diminishes, or altogether vanishes.

~

And who might this god be, whose pleasure it is to issue such commands, who takes satisfaction in their enactment? Shall war and treachery and grim assaults against the ecology — shall these be the deeds of religion? Shall they establish the god in the hearts of believers as author and keeper of creation?

However named or revered, this one, as suggested before, is himself a form of Baal. And there is no one (at least our text implies this) — no one so to declare. As yet, no prophet merits attention — no one to bear comparison with those to come. None to resist, to name the sins of the mighty, to proclaim true God, a deity utterly other than the projected idol of a criminal clan.

~

And let it be conceded: We too dwell in a world closely resembling this awful one, and its authoritarian afflictions. God help us.

~

Thus matters proceed, a kind of Cambodian or Guatemalan or Rwandan extermination scene. (Yet, placed beside the slaughters of our lifetime, this one is of modest scale.)

~

10:6-36 Jehu, a royal cynic, orders the seventy descendants of Ahab slain. The victims are decapitated. The heads are sent to him in baskets; he piles the gruesome trophies at the entrance of the city. Then he addresses the people, disavowing the murders.

Such derelictions, and those which follow, are bathed in a hideous religiosity. The "just" war is elevated to a "holy" war. Slaughter is salted with a fiery deistic impulse.

Yahweh be invoked! And the outcome is simple, inevitable: which is to say — anything goes, including mass murder and scorched-earth policy.

~

Worthy of note is this biblical implication: We of a later era hardly can lay claim to an improved conscience, whether in the behavior of authority or citizenry.

When the first Gulf slaughter was immanent, senior Bush and Hussein each invoked the god of his choice as favoring "my just cause." A witless charade, marionettes battering one another in a Punch-and-Judy show of mutual loathing. And God wept with us, in those who suffered and died, victims of the demagogues.

~

We read on, and are steeped in horror. Jehu announces a festival in honor of Baal. He assembles priests and people in the temple of the god. Straightfaced, he orders the suppliants to ensure that no worshipers of the rival deity are present. And he "advances to offer holocausts and victims."

Holocausts, victims; at a signal, the multitude of worshipers is slain on the spot, and their temple razed. Whatever battered walls stand, we are told, are used as a pissoir "to this day." In such wise, by such hands, is the "true god" vindicated.

Chapter 11

Queen or king, it matters little: ruinous. At the highest level, women and men are interchangeably wicked. It is as though each new candidate enters into a cloud of enchantment. Within, morality is suspended; a covenant with the god is stipulated as the sole rule of law.

The covenant is abruptly and sternly enforced: "no other gods before me."

The arrangement would seem to be political and ethnic rather than in any recognizable sense religious. Baals are "foreign" gods; their acceptance implies syncretism, assimilation — and to that extent, the dissolution, gradual or swift, of a people's self-understanding. Letting go the god, they lose themselves, their anchor, their story.

By dire mandate, this cannot be. In fidelity to the blood bond, the kings intrigue, betray, murder. And each remains piously stalwart in defense of the "correct god." It is like a discordant tune, played over and over by mad fingers on broken strings.

∼

Queen Athaliah is a case in point. She purposes to secure the throne by killing off the royal line. But an impediment frustrates the plot: against odds, Joash, a little prince, is snatched from her design and hidden in the temple. Then, at age seven, well-guarded, he is brought forth and crowned. And the harridan queen is taken, led outside the temple precincts, and slain.

We have seen two women rulers: Jezebel and Athaliah. Alike in criminality, the two are joined in a desolate fate.

Of what import is gender to the god of war and his vast engine, the "system"? Woman, man — the lubricant of the gears is human blood.

∼

Epitaph on a Tyrant
Perfection, of a kind, was what he was after,
And the poetry he invented was easy to understand;
He knew human folly like the back of his hand,
And was greatly interested in armies and fleets;
When he laughed, respectable senators burst with laughter,
And when he cried, the little children died in the streets.
W. H. Auden

A King's Greed, a Prophet's Epitaph (Chs. 12–13)

12:1-17

This chapter has a single, all but obsessive subject: money. As well it might — money being, so to speak, along with war and religion, a principality of note. Or shall we suggest that the triad is a kind of trinity-idol, closely conjoined, a three-in-one godling, money-war-religion?

And further, is a historical law of some note implied here? Does the trinity-idol seek (and reward) sycophants, today as well as anciently?

It seems fitting, then, that in our text a great to-do arises concerning financial arrangements of temple and priesthood. At the start, King Joash is inclined to generosity toward the priests: they receive freely the income accruing to temple and worship. In turn, the priests are held responsible for repairs of temple and environs.

The arrangement shortly grows faulty, alas. The stipends are considerable; and by one means or another, they take wing and fly far from their stated purpose, to nest in priestly pockets. Meantime, the proud temple of Solomon turns shabby with neglect. The sorry state of affairs continues uncorrected, we are told, for twenty-three years.

∾

Lord of a slum? We are told nothing of the reaction of the temple god as his dwelling deteriorates. Clearly, the system is gone to rot. Someone must intervene. Joash does so, in the form of a new decree. No more fat sacerdotal purses. Henceforth, all stipends must be applied directly to the upkeep of the temple.

Moreover, a humiliating codicil. Oversight of financial matters is removed from the priests.

And the new arrangement hums along satisfactorily, the probity of layfolk in vivid contrast to the negligence and greed of the clerical caste.

∾

12:18-22

One more episode (also concerning lucre) of this somewhat less-than-spectacular reign. King Hazael of Aram, of whom we have heard in the ominous prophecies of Elisha, launched an attack against Jerusalem. Anxious to forfend disaster, Joash decides to buy his opponent off. To that end, he empties the royal coffers of his predecessors as well as his own. More: he seizes and hands over the treasury of the temple.

And King Hazael, loot in hand, withdraws. All said, could the greedy interloper have worked a better bargain?

~

One supposes that the episode is of import to the chronicler. A put-down of the priesthood? A reminder that lucre easily turns filthy, tainting the consecrated? Or dovetailing episodes of greed, war-making, and religion, a reminder that these stand in close affinity?

In any case, the royal line is thinning out. One after another, kings, like sorry winter roses, bloom meagerly, wither, and fall. A majority lack even the will to do evil.

~

13:14-20

And the death of Elisha nears. The reigning king of Israel, another Joash, arrives, weeping over the enfeebled prophet. His outcry is a strange echo, a dying fall: "My father, my father, the chariot of Israel and its driver!"

A remarkable outcry. Years before, Elisha shouted the words as he witnessed the heavenly assumption of Elijah and donned the mantle of his mentor. Now the cry is torn from a far different throat, a kind of confession, altogether unexpected in so violent a ruler. Has Joash learned something of note? Does even such as he bear witness to the truth?

This truth: that his wars, his depredations, have worked only ill. Clearly, Elijah and Elisha are more powerful agents of the prospering of Israel than armaments or chariots of the kings.

But wait. Elisha is not yet prepared to shuffle off this mortal coil. Nor is his bellicose spirit stilled, nor his warlike imagery. He too cries out, as though in a frenzy: "Arrows! Launch them, strike the earth with them! Harder — three times is not sufficient to crush the abominable Hazael of Aram!"

And as though the fire died in that flare, Elisha expires, fury like a burning coal on his lips.

~

13:21

We are told in a single remarkable verse that, despite all, Elisha's grave is glorious. Sometime after his death, the cortège of a dead man is disrupted by brigands. Hastily they dump the corpse into the tomb of Elisha, and flee. The body touches the bones of the saint, and the dead man walks.

~

In Elisha we encounter once more a strangely uneven conscience. On occasion he speaks plainly and unequivocally; again, with a vast hemming and hawing. Sometimes boundaries are firmly set; that, or a moral void opens.

Insight and courage are his gifts. But often these go awry, or stand impeded. Then a spirit of terror and revenge erupts. And the spasm, as far as the record goes, is never reproved from on high.

What to say of Elisha, to praise or dispraise? Juggling of plain truth, guile and stonewalling, gross connivance with the powerful — these mark and mar his path in the world. He misreads the will of God with astonishing presumption — that God would speak a language of lunacy, would launch, without scruple or second thought, war upon war.

Elisha spurs on the kings and their warriors — to avenge, to redress wrongs, to praise military victory. To make of war upon war the summing up, immodest and vainglorious, of this era of kings!

~

Shall we name Elisha the king's prophet? If so, we indulge in an oxymoron, or an outright abuse of language. There is no such, there cannot be, a "king's prophet." We shall learn it as we encounter the great age of 800-500 C.E.

Prophet against king; yes — prophet contrary, contradicting. Along with all manner of mime and metaphor and acts of outright resistance.

And on the king's part: "Who will rid me? . . ." Every stratagem of humiliation and jostling about and defamation follow. And, if deemed expedient, violent death.

～

Then our man Elisha, "the king's prophet." If such a title is to be accounted a grace and an honor, so be it. All said, he is prophet to the king's advantage. A lackey, a hireling; King Henry's Cranmer, and no Thomas More. Elisha, together with his god and king, comprising a unity of brutish resolve and act.

The Spoils of War, Continued (Chs. 14, 15, 16)

These chapters continue with their brisk run-through of inconsequential rulers. A catalogue of nonachievement, of wars, the looting of treasuries, suppression, and contempt of the truth.

But wait, there is hope.

～

Be this noted, and with a deep susurration of gratitude. At long last, Isaiah appears on the scene. And he is laved in a strange — indeed, inexplicable — silence. Alas, the great prophet will be heard from in our book, but late, so late: in the reign of Hezekiah.

Can it be that he spoke earlier, but his words are expunged from these pages? Was his voice stifled because an altogether-mediocre king, Uzziah, and his unremarkable successors, Jotham and Ahaz, censored out of existence his oracles — telling, as surely they told, of the fate of tyrants?

Exile: The Final Tragedy (Ch. 17)

Disaster impends, the ruinous crest of a wave that gathered force for centuries. The crisis is carefully dated: "In the ninth year of the reign of King Hoshea. . . ."

Samaria is overwhelmed. And for two alleged defaults, the king is imprisoned. Defaults? If so, they surely imply the low status in which he and his nation are held. He is a lackey; the nation is colonized.

The royal crimes were these. He dared send envoys to Egypt, the imperial enemy. Bow and scrape, scrape and bow. And so survive.

Not enough. A bejeweled finger wags churlishly in the face of this nonentity. He failed to pay annual tribute to the king of Assyria.

Finally and at wearying length, we have come to the end, frayed and sordid, of the tales of imperialists.

~

17:7-23

All unexpected, the text is interrupted by a moral reflection. We are to know in some detail the causes of the final disaster.

Can there have occurred a leap in understanding? It is almost as though we were suddenly transposed to the era of the prophets. Does the shadow of Isaiah cross the page?

To say the least, the "almost" is a "not quite." The defaults concern matters of cult, solely. The god of Israel, as is famously known, desires no other gods impeding his rule.

But this era is notorious for other offenses, as the worse vies with the worst. Now, kings and people alike "pursued vanity, and themselves became vanity."

An old story, this worshiping of idols, a historical "original sin," old as the line of kings: golden calves at Dan and Bethel, steles, cult of the Baals, cult of the "armies of heaven," worship in "high places" and "under verdant trees." Assimilation and its symbols, in sum, and the symbols perennially hateful to the Jerusalem god and his votaries: "they followed the customs of those peoples whom the god had evicted."

And yet, and yet. The memory of their god is long, longer than the ages of default. Remember! is the command. Do not forget!

Has the god not performed great deeds on their behalf? Has he not "led them out of the land of Egypt, out from the dominion of the pharaoh"?

The chapter of faults and failings is long and detailed, and admits of many authors and revisions and borrowings, especially from Deuteronomy and Jeremiah.

~

The eye is caught and held by that "not yet." The era of the prophets has not dawned. The moral sense of the tribe is but half-formed. Niceties of cult hold first place in any collective examen of conscience.

(The single crime ascribed to the people and their kings is the sacrifice of children. But the crime is judged, if one can credit it, as solely a cultic depravity.)

Of interest too is the declaration that the god "warned Israel and Judah by every prophet and seer."

Prophets there were — an abundance of prophets, we are led to believe, since the day David was anointed by Samuel. And later, entire schools of prophecy arose in the land.

Nonetheless, a huge question remains. What did these contribute to form the conscience of kings or commoners?

～

It seems, as we have reflected, that these savants — and here one must include even Elijah and Elisha — for the most part hemmed and hawed.

We loved them; we were grateful for them. We noted as well their ambiguous stance in prospect of war. How they moved unsteadily, in a kind of limbo between throne and altar. In consequence, only now and then were they more lucid or courageous than the kings they served.

They served the kings. This, it would seem, was the rub. Such matters as injustice and war-making, neglect of the poor, fraud, murder — issues that will fairly obsess the prophets — by and large were ignored. These wise "men of god" were bystanders, non-impeders.

For ourselves, the era is a long catechumenate, and desolate. For hope and enlightenment we must wait and wait, on others.

～

Nonetheless, we give thanks for small blessings eked out in such times. The Babylonian disaster approaches; ethical realities emerge from the mist; a sense of crime and consequence grows on the air.

Granted, the crimes adduced are narrowly defined (adultery, assassination, betrayal), while other, far graver sins are hardly mentioned (war upon war, invasions, extinction of entire bloodlines).

～

We note a further development of vast moment.

On occasion the king, whatever his glory and pretension, stands un-

der judgment. In certain delicts (admittedly few), he too must acknowledge violation of moral boundaries and taboos.

Saul sins (we are unsure in what regard) and must pay up; so also David (for one sin among a multitude, equally awful or worse). And Solomon's end is pure disaster.

~

As to our story, its closure is unutterably tragic. The entire populace
must undergo a cruel, purifying hegira, a forced march and exile, ". . . far
from their country, in Assyria, where they dwell to this day."

~

17:24-27

And finally we are offered a history (much simplified, to be sure, and with
a Judean bias) of the peoples who replaced the exiles in Samaria. The account offers one version of the origin of the Samaritans.

(In his time, Jesus will encounter these fierce naysayers in the astonishing exchange with the woman at the well [John 4]. And of another Samaritan he will make a shocking point, in a parable beyond praise [Luke
10:25-37].)

~

According to the version before us, a clever imperial tactic is devised
by the king of Assyria. Troubled memories of forced eviction perdure
among the exiles. Such memories periodically threaten to erupt, endan-
gering the iron law of "things as they are."

The king is faced with a terrifying possibility. Will a sense of the
wrongs of enslavement tempt the exiles to rebellion?

To erase the dangerous memories, a draconian measure is called for.
Let the past be canceled, with its images of place (where we belong, and
shall we not return one day?), of homeland and horizon, ancestors, village, custom, feasts — the "blue remembered hills" — the savor of freedom lost.

The imperial method brutally fills a vacuum with a second exile. Another population is forcibly moved, this one into Samaria, to replace the evicted peoples.

The forced arrivals are a polyglot mix: they come from north of Babylon, Mesopotamia, Syria. Moreover — and this of utmost import — they know nothing of the "god of this land." The expression is repeated three times, perhaps an ironic commentary on superstitions that linger in Samaria after, during, even preceding the exile.

~

So, to the edict: a prime example of imperial presumption. The newly arrived must be taught to worship this "god of the land." If they are not instructed, the anger of this god will be aroused. And disaster in nature will follow (as formerly occurred, we are reminded, in an assault by lions).

Thus the rationale for a "religious" mandate; a primitive regression indeed, and stark.

In point of fact, the Asssyrian emperor's concern is grossly political. Like every tyrant, he must induce calm amid the conquered, whether in the land of exile or the former homeland. And what better pacifier than a menu laced with soporific "religion"?

~

17:28

Placate the god, then, who in turn will pacify the people.

A priest-exile is brought back to the homeland. This one (anonymous, perhaps deliberately so) is crucial to the designs of the Assyrians. He knows his role: he is a missionary of sorts.

He is also, of course, a "mole," an emissary of empire. He sets to evangelizing the pagans as to correct rites and the perils of misbehavior.

The god of the exiles, as we recall, was fiercely tribal: he was "god of the land." So, of necessity, the religion of the Samaritans will be tribal.

(We note, gratefully, the contrary, generous vision of Isaiah. "All nations" are included in the ambit of divine love [ch. 2 and passim].)

~

17:41

A shadow is cast upon the future (upon ourselves!) by the concluding verse: "Thus this people reverenced Yahweh. Still, they paid tribute to their gods. And their children and the children of their children continue to this day, the behavior of their ancestors."

Schizophrenia of the spirit: in practice and behavior, servitude to this or that idol.

~

As for ourselves, let us confess. We are heirs of the Promise — and of the Betrayal as well.

Dawn at Last: Isaiah and the Last Days of Empire

(Chs. 18–25)

*The great Hebrew prophets presuppose a world full of big chances; they are
on the lookout for contingencies — a world in which breaks are possible,
whether in the symmetry or the strict sequence of time. Linear time, that
unwavering symbol of a stable order, cannot hold against the onslaughts of
God's will.*

*For the prophets, therefore, imagination takes precedence over the
sheerly factual, "what must be" takes priority over "what is." The universe
must yield place not only to the laws of large numbers and immemorial
tradition, but also to minorities of one or more that subvert a ruling order.*

*There must be time and space, that is to say, not only for the indicative
mood of what is everlastingly the case, but also for the subjunctive and imperative moods of what might be, could be, and must be — the reign of
God — against all the odds.*

Equivalently, this is to demand that the universe be sacramental. . . .

David Toolan, S.J.,
"Spiritualities in a Post-Einsteinian Universe"

~

The Great Lie of hell is: There is no heaven. More: put the same matter in a brutal imperative. There can be no heaven.

Historically, the Lie is variously enacted. In Egypt it went this way:
There is no Moses. There can be none. And in the era of Kings: There is

no Isaiah. There cannot be. This is the flattest of indicative modes, the politesse of power.

The words may be honeyed, implied, laved in innuendo. But the underpinning is ironbound, imperative. There can be no Moses, no Isaiah. Or, if such dare appear, they shall be disposed of. We all but hear the muffled drumbeat, the edict of Kings, which is to say, of the Realm of Necessity.

Something is allowed, however. Shall it be a kind of "venting voice"? Well, why not? Let there be such as Elisha and Nathan. These minor objectors to the system ("things as they are") — their reservations will be duly recorded; written on water, so to speak. Nods of respect will greet them, placations, attentive ears. And nothing will change, not a whit.

(And in our own time: there can be no Oscar Romero or Martin Luther King. Or, if such appear, we shall dispose of them. Meantime, make do with the likes of Billy Graham or Jesse Jackson.)

Hezekiah: King of Contradiction (Ch. 18)

18:1-16

There arrives on the scene of generational disarray a king Hezekiah. On him from the start, much praise is lavished. "He put his trust in the LORD, the God of Israel; and neither before him nor after him was there anyone like him among all the kings of Judah."

Well. We shall see (and great Isaiah shall say)* how the king measures up to the estimate, self-estimate or scribal — or perhaps the two, coming to the same thing?

~

In any case, for the first time in a tormented eon, a sublime relief dawns. We have witnessed an eon of intransigent wars and alarms, have encountered the kings and their works and pomps — the great among them (few or none), the run of the mill (most), and the actively wicked (distressingly numerous).

---

* Chapters 18–20 are a reprise of Isaiah 38–39.

~

And now at last, amid the fog and welter we name history — even dare name sacred history — amid intrigue, violence, and treachery — out of the darkness Isaiah comes, a giant in dwarfland, a seer among the blind, the prophet and poet.

We have murmured again and again: O world, too much with us. And now: Glory be, such relief!

~

One after another came the kings, and now and again, a queen. They were stale of mind, occupied with prosaic — not to say bureaucratic, not to say morally hideous — "affairs of state." We were told of an exception, David, a harpist and composer of songs. But his efforts were limited indeed: he laid sweet (and of necessity passing) relief on the chills and fevers of King Saul. Which ambiguous figure, together with his pathologies, all but summed up the era. And hardly upward to the likes of David and Solomon.

But then, but then. Our Isaiah appears in the text — a tardy arrival, to be sure. Too late to stem the tide of catastrophe? We shall see.

~

The early phases of the reign of Hezekiah are a puzzle. He seems to have restored Yahwism, which had all but gone up in Baalist incense.

Still, in light of the king's highly unpredictable behavior, how explain a passage like the following? "He rebelled against the king of Assyria, and refused to serve him."

In a far different tradition, Hezekiah seems to have met the Assyrian threat with a quivering terror. One of his gestures is pure appeasement. He strips the temple and palace treasury and sends the loot off to the rival dynast. And along with the booty, a note. Its message could hardly, by the wildest hyperbole, be called "rebellious": "I have done wrong; depart from me, and I will pay whatever you impose on me."

~

Difficult, too, in light of dire events, to justify the flat statement: "He succeeded in all he undertook."

During the siege of Jerusalem, against the will of Yahweh he fortified the city — a calamitous decision. Then he cravenly summoned the prophet; in effect, "Go, placate the deity."

Are we to name such expediencies "success"? We are puzzled, and led to speculate. Could it be that as our scribe sets down these encomia, the eye of a tyrant peers over his shoulder?

In which case, puzzlement is hardly lessened. Could not the chronicler set down a consistent account — even a falsely consistent one? In whose interest, one wonders, such contradicting stories?

~

Or perhaps this: a species of deconstruction is at work. Are we being led by crooked lines to a straight conclusion? Perhaps the tortuous accounts point to a double tradition. The first would have the king peerless in judgment and act. The second makes of him a Hamlet, floundering about as the Assyrian tyrant approaches.

In any case, nothing of the temple riches is safe from this royal pacifier. He rips apart the jambs and uprights of the great doors, strips them of gold, and ships them off.

Ten years pass. Asssyria grows restive once more. How to respond? Hezekiah is stuck between a rock and a hard place. He is preoccupied in making (one thinks: rather panicky) overtures toward Egypt, as a frontal defense against his nemesis.

But does he imagine that the Assyrians have no eyes and ears, and know nothing of his attempts to shore up the would-be empire of Judah?

~

18:17-37

An Assyrian delegation arrives in Jerusalem. The message is menacing, apodictic, a prime sample of imperial rhetoric: "On what do you base this confidence of yours? Do you imagine that words, launched on empty air, are a substitute for strategy and might in warfare?"

And they ridicule the Egyptian connection: "Egypt is a broken reed; it will pierce the hand of the one who leans on it."

The contempt and arrogance are breathtaking. The trust of the Judeans in their god, it appears to the enemy, is a bootless fantasy. Reliance on Yahweh will bring no benefit.

In the breach, the deity will prove as helpless as the Egyptians (or, for that matter, as their gods) to save.

~

In point of fact, we learn that Yahweh has abruptly chosen sides — but this time, hardly in favor of his "chosen." A terrible judgment against Jerusalem is to befall — and this at the hands of pagans. A turning of tables, a truly astonishing reversal of fortune — the darling of the divine eye has been unchosen.

The Asssyrian invasion proceeds, ineluctable — and this by command of Yahweh and no other. The order to destroy the holy city is signed, sealed, and delivered to — goys.

And more. For the first time, Yahweh makes of a pagan ruler his oracular mouthpiece. An epiphany, to a pagan? At the least, it would seem, a revelation, a word.

And received, acted upon, taken seriously. Quite beside himself with rancorous pride, the king of Assyria glories in the charge given him: "Yahweh it was who said to me: 'Go up and destroy that land.'"

Whose god, whose side taken? In the entire Hebrew bible, we have heard nothing to match this.

~

No empty vaunt of the tyrant. The pronunciamento of Yahweh, his choice of pagans to defeat the recalcitrants of his own household, is verified by no less an authority than Isaiah.

According to the prophet, Yahweh speaks:

Woe to Assyria,
my rod in anger,
my staff in wrath.

Against
an impious nation
I send him.

In wrath of spirit
I command —

seize, plunder,
carry off loot —

tread them down
like mud
of the streets!

(But this, alas, was hardly Yahweh's intent . . .)

"My hand reached out
toppling
idolatrous kingdoms. . . .

Shall I not wreak
the like

against
Jerusalem,

her
images

foul,
befouling?"

Isaiah 10:5-7, 10-11

Isaiah: Prophet of Hope against Hope (Ch. 19)

19:3-13

At length the king and counselors send for Isaiah.

Too late? It is desperately late, as the uneasy delegation admits dolefully: "This is a day of chastisement, agony, and opprobrium. The children have come to term, and there is no strength to bring them forth."

Isaiah is equal to the moment. The message to Hezekiah, his knees uncontrollably knocking, is curt and to the point.

At the same time, for the Assyrian upstart the prophet includes nothing of comfort. The aggressor will be forced to withdraw from the siege, and his end will be dire.

~

Puzzlement again. From the purport of the message, it would seem that Yahweh is of two minds. On the one hand, the god (according to the Assyrians) has rejected the chosen and embraced the Assyrians. It is the goys who will prevail.

And yet — double mind, double bind? The enemy of my enemy, my friend? Yahweh, it appears, cannot come to a settled mind. Momentously he shifts loyalties. It is as though the tides of seven oceans had turned in an hour, swamping.

He rejects the chosen, even as he despises their mortal enemies. In good time he will deal harshly with the imperialists at the gate.

We are deep in a tangle of logic.

~

Logic tangled, even on high? Those invaders — they have uttered (equivalent, if somewhat puzzling) "blasphemies" against Yahweh. Presumably the (somewhat confused) reasoning goes thus: Only the deity is allowed to pronounce, in the ear of pagans, threats against the idolaters of his own household.

The claim of the goys, that they are subjects of divine favor, is genuine. Nonetheless, let the claim be kept secret, seems the implication. Let not the Assyrians dare repeat at large that they are the chosen sword of justice against Jerusalem.

Yet the claim of the Assyrians, we note, is reported also by Isaiah.

Surely this is a complex divinity, unpredictable and unsettling. Who shall name him their champion and not shake in their boots?

~

Another passage parallels the above. According to this version, a letter, rather than a delegation, is dispatched to King Hezekiah. Small matter the difference; the sour tone abides.

The message: Let it be known to the foolhardy that other nations, despite the intervention of their gods, have fallen before Assyrian might. And is it to be imagined that Jerusalem shall prove an exception?

~

19:14-20

The king peruses the letter, with what plunge of spirit may well be imagined. Then he takes resolve, and mounts to the temple to pray.

Unexpectedly, his petition proves admirable, flooded with fond summoning of the works of Yahweh. And one is led to speculate: was it composed by Isaiah himself?

~

At long last, rejoicing speeds the heart's pace. Isaiah and his like walk the earth, towering over a pigmy eon. At long last, the earth grows resplendent with grand prophecy.

In the historical books — whether Joshua, Judges, or Samuel — we have seen the worst. And in Maccabees we shall see the worst doubled and trebled. The worst of us humans and our systems — and yes, the worst of the god.

~

Our Bible, like a Virgil guiding Dante, has conducted us through the mire and fury of our common history. A tale we long to disclaim, to shed like a garment befouled. And we cannot.

Appalling is this genealogy. We are shown the infamy to which we humans can descend — worse, have descended. (And shall descend?)

It is as though the creation of hell on earth were the sworn purpose of empire. As though God had yielded the field of creation to a coven of demons.

~

As though, as though. As though the deity were a lapsarian god, sunk in despair at human follies, determined, along with brutal collaborators, to bring down the primal covenant, that pillar of creation, restored after Fall and Flood.

We have seen and suffered through all this. Now, welcome to — God. To whom in reverence, at long last, we apply a Capital Letter. God, so tardily on the scene of God's word. God, succeeding the witless, willful scene of the godless gods.

Thanks be to God, to whom we lay claim at last, the sole legitimate claim, the claim that heavily exacts faith. And thanks as well to God's stupendous servant, Isaiah, son of Amoz.

~

The prayer of Hezekiah. Let us grant the king this: he may have composed the prayer. It may be that the spirit of Isaiah so permeated temple and palace that a king may pray like a prophet. When an Isaiah dwells in the world, no miracle but may be.

The themes of the prayer are worth recording: praise, the truth of memory, humble suppliance. This, in sum:

We are helpless; you are all-powerful. Unworthy as we are, turn to us a kind eye. Please, one more time. For at the hour of the first creation, you chose in favor of life. Your breath lay upon the void and stirred it to life, even to us, the living.

And again you chose, delivering us from tyrannical Egypt.

Deliver us anew, we pray. The Assyrians utter blasphemies; they liken you, our God, to the gods of the nations, their idols of stone and wood. Resist them; rebuke them. Succor the remnant who cry out to you.

~

Isaiah, that clairvoyant spirit, man of Yahweh, approves the prayer. So does God. And in awe, we take note of the sea change. How slowly, painfully, Another, a Transcendence, a Someone not of this world and of this world (but not of this world in the gross way of the kings) — how Someone is emerging from the shadows, from the monstrous simulacra set in memory and text by rulers and their chroniclers. A Someone is emerging from the fantasies of necromancers, from the closet of imperial history, where the dead are forbidden speech and the living oftener than not utter lies.

Someone; not "a god." Not "one of the gods." God. Who this Yahweh is.

Who. Yahweh.

The transcendent Event has come to pass through Isaiah and his kind. They have welcomed the Creator, Savior, our only Hope.

~

The people walked in darkness for centuries. The bravado and slummish conscience of judges and kings and their cronies testified again and again, despite all protestation to the contrary: Yahweh? We know nothing of Yahweh!

The Kings knew nothing of Yahweh. Through their hirelings, the historians and priests and court prophets, they offered only a brutal and deceptive event — this or that intervention of a god among the gods. A god who was a mirror image, all said, of themselves and their criminality.

Solomon installed the idol in a grand sanctuary and called it god. The act was pure dementia gloriae.

~

The god bore their own moral physiognomy, a mirror image of low contrivance. Solomon welcomed the image, offered it a royal dwelling — first of all in the royal mind.

In accord with the sterile letter of the law, kings and priests obeyed the law that forbade images of the deity. There was no "image" in the temple.

And simultaneously, they disobeyed. The "images" reigned in their mind: foul means, befouled appetite, cruelty, violence. Enthroned there.

~

19:21-28

Isaiah, prince among poets, celebrating hope against hope. What a gift he is. How he restores and raises the spirit, invoking an utterly new reality — the possibility of grace and goodness, even in such as ourselves. More:

learn of him, the exemplar. A grand prophet embodies in himself both grace and goodness.

We catch the song. In these dour pages named for the Kings, in this vile handbook of the methods and mores of "dwellers on the earth" — a new song is raised. It celebrates purification of spirit, the cleansing of historic follies and their filth from hands and feet and heart.

Isaiah. Who bears no resemblance, in ethos or behavior, to the kings, their military commanders and counselors. Who is "capax veritatis," who speaks the truth — and allows, even welcomes the consequence. (Is not royal consequence, he will reason, proof that the truth has cut to the imperial bone?)

~

Isaiah and his God break into song. The theme is denunciation of the enemy, Sennacherib the Assyrian:

They despise you,
laugh you to scorn,

behind your back
they mock you,
daughters of Jerusalem!

Whom then
do you dare insult,
ignorant freebooter,

against whom
lift heel?

None other
than the Holy One!

You said:
"My chariots
mount the heights,

"my blade brings low
those regal crests —
cedar and cypress, down!

"I drink deep
the elixir
of fabled streams;

"with scorching breath
I dry, dry, dry up —
tributaries of Egypt!"

Listen, attend to me.

This, long ages ago,
I, Yahweh, brought to pass,
all ordained beforehand —

that you
reduce to an ash
fortified proud cities,

their inhabitants
scattered, confounded,

vanishing like a smoke,
like grass of the fields
powdered by cruel sirocco.

My doing, not yours —

your breath, your bravado
under my gaze, my judgment.

Insolence
offends my ears —

Hear this, great marauder:

Harmless as a midnight moth
you flit in, flutter out,
wayward, evanescent —

darkness
drinking the dark.

Sennacherib,
great tawny-flanked bull(y),
I shall tan your hide, flay you,

shall fashion
from leathern pelt
thongs, sandals of my feet.

But first.
I fasten
a ring in your nose,
a bit in your jaws,

ride you hither and yon
at my sweet will —
a beast for show —

lead you back and back
until dark Nineveh
owns you utterly —

you
darkness
swallowed by darkness.

～

It is pure Isaiah, this scalding put-down of arrogance.

(An example also, and an invitation: that we too take a long, skeptical, even scornful glance at authorities who would amortize our conscience, bending us to their brutish ends, their wars, their insolence and lies.)

Isaiah is prophet of the great refusal. A prophet, as goes without saying, who practiced what he preached.

~

19:29-31

Our vatic one also offers a word of hope to shuffling, benighted King Hezekiah:

> Let this be your sign:
>
> In the first year,
> no harvest;
>
> borrow
> from granaries.
>
> In the second,
> austerity;
>
> gather
> the gleanings.
>
> In the third,
> plant once more,
> and harvest!
>
> See,
> roots hold firm,
>
> and above —
>
> a heavy tassel
> dances in the wind.
>
> To the holy city,
> look — a remnant
> comes,

bearing sheaves
in triumph.

Our Yahweh

works
this
wonder!

~

Not a "literal" sign, to be sure — if such an oxymoron can be thought
to exist. A word of hope, of hope against hope. Dark as the times are (and
the darkness is to be confessed, within and without, the sin, betrayal,
contempt of God's hope) — still, against all odds, life and love assert
themselves, and prevail.

Isaiah sings it in a rush of poetic fervor — more, he lives by it, this
outrageous hope. Lives by the very hope of God. Whose Name, as centuries pass and sin proliferates, must be named and named anew — Hope
against Hope.

~

In the dark times shall there be singing?

Yes.
There will be singing
about the dark times.

Bertolt Brecht

~

19:32-34

Finally, another oracle against the tyrant at the ramparts:

Like a matchwood,
his bow is broken,

no arrow sped,
never a battlement won,

no pennant
lodged in our soil.

See him
in shame
fall back.

For David's sake,
for very love,
see —

city, valley, mountain —

like
the newborn

cherished

in my

two
hands.

~

19:35-37

And shortly, a providential outcome, as Isaiah predicted. We are in the
realm of popular myth. An "angel of the LORD" smites the Asssyrians.
Perhaps a decimating plague? In any case, in speedy disarray the survi-
vors withdraw. The siege is broken.

The dossier closes. The Assyrian tyrant, worshiping in a temple of
Nineveh, is assassinated by his own sons.

Sic transit gloria. Et sic res solvitur. Thus the glory dissolves. And
thus the mortal threat dissipates.

~

King Hezekiah emerges from these pages robed in his true colors — gray, jaundice? — in any case, hardly the guise of a hero, hands steady at the helm of state. Hardly. Yet one grants this: he set in motion a strenuous religious reform, spurred by the discovery of the lost text of Deuteronomy.

Still, far from a hero: in the days of siege, an ambiguous role led him again and again into conflict with Isaiah.

All said, this Hezekiah is a sedulous ape of the great powers. The enemy approached. The king lowered weapons from the wall of Solomon's gallery, the grand "Forest of Lebanon." The intention was clear: violent resistance in face of violence.

Then, further steps: he fortified the city and diverted the waterworks to ensure supplies during the siege. For these machinations, Isaiah rebuked him in fury: "You took no note of the city's Maker, nor did you consider the One who built it long ago."

The intent of the mysterious rune seems clear. Before our eyes the god of Hezekiah is transformed: a dazzling butterfly emerges from a millennial cocoon. Astonished, we ponder the newborn (or twice-born) Deity.

Eccolo! God, counseling an altogether new spirit and tactic: nonviolence.

The command is unmistakable; it is also unique. Rare, so rare in biblical record. A command is issued from above, and a king's military designs are halted in their tracks. Hezekiah is commanded, in sum, to renounce the tit for tat of his ancestors, of his own genetic leanings.

A momentous implication. The king who prepares for war is disobedient to the will of the Holy.

A Puzzle of Praise for a Foolish King (Ch. 20)

The siege was lifted. Isaiah was convinced the reversal occurred by divine intervention. Sometime after, Hezekiah was stricken with mortal illness. Bedridden, the king wept like a frightened child. Dread of mortality?

To the childish let us be forbearing. Isaiah hastens to the royal bedside; he bears a mitigating word from Yahweh. "O king, dry your tears; an earlier decree of demise is canceled. You shall enjoy fifteen additional years in this mortal coil."

~

20:7-11

The prophet is skilled in pharmaceutical remedies; for comfort of the distempered royal parts, he concocts a poultice of figs. Shortly, signs of recovery appear. The worst, it would seem, is over.

But only for a time. Shortly his highness grows petulant — a good omen and a bad. He demands a portent, assurance of the truth of his healing.

And we all but hear the sigh of Isaiah. The prophet seems condemned to serve in a royal nursery. Must every mood of this great child be indulged?

Nevertheless. A sign the king seeks, a sign he shall have — as evanescent and childish as himself. This: on a palace staircase, shadows gambol forward, then backward. A symbol of the king's moody self?

How patient is our Isaiah with this blubberer!

~

20:12-21

More foolishness. Hezekiah receives a delegation of Babylonians. From afar, they bear largesse and good wishes. Trojans bearing gifts? Isaiah judges so. The king dissents. In a foolish gesture he conducts a tour of the palace, pointing grandly to treasures of silver and gold, weaponry and food supplies. It is all quite silly — and somewhat endearing too: Who can be angry at the antics of adolescence?

~

The inspection continues, the Babylonians all but laughing up their sleeves. If wishes were horses. . . . Hezekiah, a Tom Thumb, ruler of a tiny realm, dreams a vast dream: he would be emperor of a great kingdom, a very Babylon. Royal demagoguery, no more.

For relief, this can be adduced. Kings dream dreams of power and might. Let them do so. Despite themselves, they serve, foils for the spiritual nobility of others.

This is pure subversion in our text, and in the prophetic witness the text arises from. The kings are beside the point of the history they walk in. Biblical books may be named for them, but the true protagonists are the Isaiahs.

~

With Isaiah and his noble company, the prophets have entered biblical history. A new order is in place; it bespeaks compassion, gentleness, fiery truth, an end to murder as the chief instrument of power.

And a far different deity appears.

As for the kings, they are stripped of credibility; their credentials grow shabby (indeed, they always were). Then the truth shines, an epiphany: these rulers are anomalies, stuck in place, in the past, in war-making and greed and hatred; in "likeness to the nations."

~

Hezekiah frets and pouts and demands a childish "sign" to soften the onset of mortality. To such as him, death was a chief instrument of rule. But when death knocked at his door, it wore a face of Medusa, and his knees turned to whey.

~

We are granted inklings of a chief task of prophecy: a raw energy of soul that unmasks, deflates, disconcerts. The tone of the historical books changes; we are done with the court scribes, those acolytes and propagandists.

Now for a dose of the bitter truth. Let us read of a sniveling king who takes to his couch and whines for relief — from the likes of Isaiah. And a bitter relief is proffered: the truth, long ignored and despised. It is like a poultice laid on the sores of an impending "second death." Talk about subversion.

~

This Hezekiah, for his part, is master of the faux pas compounded. Thanks to his misguided guided tour, the Babylonians return home with a firsthand appraisal of the resources of their rival.

Isaiah grimly confronts the king. What, he demands stormily, has gone on here? He bears an announcement: Yahweh is angered at the king's charade of worldly force and wealth.

Let foolish Hezekiah know it: a day of accounting nears. The treasury will be looted, swept away. And the beneficiaries? The Babylonians he has cosseted. Worse; his own sons will be seized, emerging as eunuchs of the king of Babylon.

~

Does the dire pronouncement disturb or chasten? It does not. The king responds airily: "Why, the word you bring is in no way unfavorable."

Someone, possibly Isaiah himself, is privy to the king's self-consoling, self-aggrandizing inner life. Hezekiah concludes the exchange with a kind of bleak self-satisfaction. After me, the deluge. So be it, but after me.

~

And our original puzzlement returns. How explain, in light of the foregoing, the praise that from the start of his reign has laved Hezekiah in divine approval? What basis for this inflated praise, reminiscent of that granted David himself?

One ventures this: the praise is due to the king's campaign against the gods that so plague Yahweh. Hezekiah, we recall, "removed the high places, shattered the pillars, and cut down the sacred poles."

And this: "He put his confidence in Yahweh. No king of Judah was comparable to him. He remained attached to Yahweh, without ever turning aside from him. . . ."

Is more than one tradition set down here? One surmises so.

Later, Isaiah has bitter reason to accuse the king of just such "turning aside." Yet the text includes this: "Yahweh was with him, and he succeeded in all his undertakings."

All his undertakings? The fortifications he raised in Jerusalem, contrary to the will of the god? His resolve to undertake violent resistance? The preferences of Yahweh vis-à-vis us humans are peculiar indeed. (Another favorite, we recall, was David. He played rascal, and worse.)

Or perhaps, as often in these stories, the suggestion is sound: we are privy to more than one tradition, a muddle of memories. Set them down, then, the bitter and mordant, the inconsistent and unpersuasive. The power that corrupts often succeeds in corrupting memory as well.

Thus, by implication, honoring the perspicacity of the prophets.

Innocent Blood on Royal Hands (Ch. 21)

Hezekiah, in any case, was succeeded by his son Manasseh. Step by step (or, when required, precipitously), this eminence undid the godly works of his father. Everything abominable in the eyes of Yahweh reappeared; ruthlessly and thoroughly, the reform was crushed.

But an awful judgment is leveled against this monster: "He spilled innocent blood, inundating Jerusalem."

Jewish tradition states that great Isaiah was among the many who perished under the blade of Manasseh. Awful, and yet befitting: a keeper of God's word dies at the hands of a renegade.

~

How much we owe Isaiah and his tradition — this genius of the spirit whose images fashion a tradition of centuries and impregnated the heart and speech of Christ.

Announcing his ministry in the synagogue of Nazareth, Jesus opened the scroll to Isaiah (61:1-2) and read: "Yahweh has sent me to bring glad tidings to the poor, to proclaim liberty to captives, recovery of sight to the blind and release to prisoners. To announce a year of favor from the Lord" (Luke 4:18-19).

We salute this towering spirit; with full hearts we thank our Isaiah. Christ's Isaiah, and our own.

~

The royal bloodline thins out — and none too soon, one sighs, for patience's sake. We ask our soul: What interest do these latter-day rulers evoke, preposterous as they are, or lethal, or both?

If they are rewarded as "virtuous," it is for a cribbed virtue indeed. In wars they vindicate a perennially touchy Yahweh. Just, the conflicts pay tribute to the god. Or so it is adduced.

And if the same rulers are condemned, it is on like grounds: they infuriate the truculent deity with works of regression and transgression — the latter invariably of a "religious" sort. They fall to the unthinkable, the intolerable: idolatry. Until Isaiah, they seldom or never confront or invoke true God, the God of compassionate love toward the poor and victimized.

These latter-day kings are, one and all, a type: a wearying succession of clones. Their delicts, their wars and crimes, in concert with the moods and frowns of their deity, lie heavy on the text. Crime, and rarely consequence. A nightmare.

And perhaps meant to be so. For our instruction.

～

The books of Samuel offered a lightless void, a world without prophecy, a people groaning under the heel of charlatan-rulers. And these later episodes, the books of Kings, prove no less awful.

This is the sum of it: prophets or no, Isaiah or no, the kings of Israel sit firm in the saddle of history. Obsessed with self-interest, conquest, greed, and betrayal, they pay small heed to the holy ones and their oracles. Deuteronomic morality is reduced to a single commandment: honor Yahweh; no strange gods. Thus a certain brand of religion offers to a mordant system a shady credential.

The system grinds on in the face of good sense and the common good. It removes the innocent and vulnerable, destroys ecology and the goods of earth. The rich grow richer; the poor languish. The inequity is as old as the era of Solomon. Its roots are lodged in the Davidic time.

～

Then, an intervention, and we take heart.

Let us celebrate the good news with a muted alleluia, as new voices are raised and a piercing vision dissipates the dark. For the first time in our tormented history, a passionate "No" unmasks and condemns an obtuse, violent, pharaonic system. The "No" is unequivocal, in debt to no worldly power.

It is as though the prophets took in hand a royal sword and fashioned it into a plowshare. A telling mime, as moral connections are forged —

between domestic misery and war and preparation for war. War, they cry, wastes the earth, creates "widows and orphans," breeds only another round of bloodletting.

The outcry saves all, saves right reason.

But what of the kings — do they hearken and obey? Seldom, if ever.

~

In the year of election 1996, Mr. Clinton signed into law a ruinous "welfare bill." It stipulated that the federal government bow out of responsibility toward the poor — especially toward the most vulnerable: the aged, the ill, the children. A week later, he signed a bill authorizing a Pentagon budget for the year ahead. The loot was excessive, far beyond the amount sought by the generals.

And the pundits pontificated: It is hardly expedient that in an election year, the candidate show himself "soft on defense."

These are but the latest in a long series of betrayals of the common good. On every point of conflict with the "lawmakers," a timorous, servile president yielded. No contest, no appeal to those who urged a contrary course — the churches, the labor unions, the homeless and unemployed — all of whose support he could have counted on.

Let this be set down as a kind of obituary. In his years in office, Clinton became a figure consistent only for ideals betrayed. A waste.

~

Another example of the like. In the weeks following the above moves, in face of a questionable provocation and without the least diplomatic effort, Clinton approved the launching of Mohawk missiles against Iraq. This he had done before. War abroad, domestic misery. And neither of these dire realities, be it noted, was mentioned in the electioneering of either party.

The conclusion seems inescapable and dire: as a political force or an inducement to compassion, the poor and homeless simply do not exist. Nor do the dying children of Iraq. And the Pentagon, that stupendous parasite, battens greatly.

Thus is underscored — if indeed we required instruction — a politics of violence, contempt, and despair.

~

In the words of Isaiah, we Americans are at the mercy of "a harsh master" (19:4). We behold a system which demands "human souls" (Rev. 18:13).

~

To our narrative. Oriental alliances, we are told, were often sealed and placed in the shrine of the god. In like manner, the Decalogue was solemnly placed in its repository, the ark of the covenant.

And what of the famous, fabulous book named Deuteronomy? Tradition told this: the scroll was placed in the temple of Jerusalem. It was subsequently hidden or lost. Or perhaps during the hideous reign of Manasseh, it was simply forgotten.

The price exacted by that loss, measured by the (surely imperfect) understanding of the times, was nearly total. The gods of death once more seized the reins of history.

The Scroll: Restored for Good? (Chs. 22–23)

22:8-13

Then, at long last, the scroll was recovered.

The scroll, as we have seen, included narrow rulings concerning worship of Yahweh. In this, Deuteronomy stood in stark contrast with the prophets and their passionate sense of neighbor, of justice, of the sins of the mighty.

The loss of the scroll — shall we name it a minor loss, in contrast to the neglect and fading of covenant? And the discovery — shall it be a partial triumph at best?

~

And what, we wonder, would have been the reaction of Isaiah to the reform set in motion by Hezekiah?

Of vastly greater import, a further question: Why did the legacy of

Isaiah disappear from the royal agenda — those matters of justice and peace and universal salvation that so consumed the prophet? His influence diminished, then vanished from the ruling ethic of his times.

Vanished, banished from the ruling ethic? Only from that exalted, corrupt sector. Elsewhere, at the edge, a sublime tradition took root.

~

22:14-20

An otherwise unknown prophetess, Huldah, rises. In contrast to Isaiah, she reinforces the dictates of Deuteronomy and its obsessive insistence on liturgical Yahwism.

A hypothesis is suggested. If Yahweh is concerned only with submission to his empery, if worship is the sole issue, why the dissenting cry of the prophets? Again and again they insist that faith in Yahweh implies more than "one God, no gods before me."

That, of course. And more, vastly more. Faith, they insist, is an eminently practical matter: it is anchored in time and this world; it enlists hearts and minds in works of justice and compassion. Faith is eminently consequential, a blessed laying on of hands — on the neighbor, the stranger at the gate, the creation itself. Choosing to be chosen by the God of life, one chooses on behalf of life and the living.

The soul of faith is enfleshed. Faith demands, insists on, an ethic in which "good works" are honored.

~

When, by what means, did this eruption of insight to all intents vanish from our text? Was Isaian teaching in fact lost to the ages to come? By the time of King Josiah and the death of Isaiah, were the words of the prophet a dead letter?

We cannot say with certainty; but the subsequent behavior of kings and people alike offers scant evidence of prophetic influence. The counsels fell silent; people and creation itself were left to the untender mercies of a royal line, one following another, plain wreckers.

~

Waiting

Face to face? Ah, no
God: such language falsifies
the relation. Nor side by side,
nor near you, nor anywhere
in time and space.
  Say you were,
when I came, your name
vouching for you, ubiquitous
in its explanations. The
earth bore and they reaped:
God, they said, looking
in your direction. The wind
changed; over the drowned
body it was you
they spat at.
  Young
I pronounced you. Older
I still do, but seldomer
now, leaning far out
over an immense depth, letting
your name go and waiting,
somewhere between faith and doubt,
for the echoes of its arrival.

R. S. Thomas

~

23:1-25

The text of Deuteronomy was recovered, we note. Momentous. The occasion demanded a conclusion, a summing up. So a prophetess came forward, proposing a solemn ritual. Let the king himself read the text aloud, and let all respond with an oath, swearing to obey "the commands, instructions and laws" thereby promulgated.

All said, it amounted at best to a partial restoration. The ethics of the time remained gravely delinquent, due beyond doubt to the pernicious influence of Manasseh. The books of Jeremiah, Zephaniah, and Ezekiel, in a torrid testimony, tell of a widespread, practical paganism in Judah.

~

Officially, praise and vast claims of success lent a halo to the successive reforms, especially those of Hezekiah. But the opposite drift, once underway, grew stronger by the year: gravity pulled, and always downward.

Life was a moonless night, befogged. The gods gathered force, enlisting their "armies of heaven," the vast apparatus of a culture of death.

~

What of Josiah, that intriguing figure? We conjure him — upright, bold, obeisant, adroit. He senses the moment and turns events to the advantage of reform. First he breaks the foreign grasp on Judah. Then cannily he takes note that Assyrian control of the northern kingdom is weakening.

Passionate for reform, the regal iconoclast moves his forces into Bethel and reclaims part of the old Israeli landhold there, smashing and burning idols as he advances.

And we are left with many a hiatus. And questions. If the reform of Josiah stood firm as claimed, why did matters so quickly deteriorate after his death — to a point literally of no return?

~

23:26-27

The god is at center stage; anger flames out uncontrolled. Have some claimed to "renew the alliance"? They succeed only in betrayal.

Light amid the Kings' Dark Legacy (Chs. 24–25)

Now come the years of shame, of near extinction and despair.

The grandeur of the Solomonic years is pulled down like a rotten tapestry. The holy city and the temple are destroyed; a first human wave is driven into exile.

Finito, all that glory.

Nebuchadnezzar first culls the notables of Jerusalem — the king, ministers, officers, skilled workmen. These, for the soundest of imperial reasons, are deported. Their skills will be put to work, enhancing the glory of Babylon.

Left behind, also for sound imperial reasons, is a detritus: the unskilled and poor. And how avoid a dire implication? There existed in the city of David (and quite taken for granted) an impoverished, unskilled, unproductive class. By implication, the "reform" of Josiah left such as these stark and stuck.

To shorten a dolorous tale, Jerusalem is sacked, the temple pulled down, a rubble. Then a final roundup. Those left behind in the earlier levy are herded off, the only exception being a small number of "workers and vine dressers."

Thus with a whimper ends the saga of the Kings, the dolors and caprices and crooked lines of imperial behavior.

And a further question: How shall God, or ourselves, write straight; what grand design may we salvage, and trace and retrace in the dust — for sake of the unborn, and indeed of ourselves?

~

To the bitter jot, the perspicacity of Samuel, announced at the start of the regal venture, is verified. This dire word: the rulers you lust after will turn on you, will assault your humanity, enslave and wreck you (1 Sam. 8:11-18).

Then, grand pageantry met our eyes. We saw the god installed in a temple, cosseted and captive, a ventriloquist of imperial ego. We saw the royal charade reach its apogee in Solomon, as "rules and mandates" were set firmly in place. Worldly systems hardened, sclerotic. A game, a wicked one, was underway, and given time, flourished. Its name: victimizer and victimized.

The Sun King died; the Solomonic "system" rolled on with fierce, uncontrolled momentum: the war engine, the piratical economics. For some, vast wealth; for the poor, contempt and neglect.

~

There came an interruption. A stick was driven in the chariot spokes of empire. The impediment was thrust in place by the hands of prophets, the great disequilabrists of self-interest and murder. They denounced the old order as inept, intolerable. They defended and cherished the poor, challenged and rebuked the oppressors.

To Isaiah and his like, all praise.

~

La lucha continua. Therefore, a midrash on Kings.

> Its goal is always a practical application to the present . . . in such a way that it gives light and direction to the generation which writes the midrash.
>
> John McKenzie, *Dictionary of the Bible*

~

We Americans are, alas, a 9/11 generation, an Afghanistan war generation, a second-Iraq-war generation. The wars go on, without end or issue, our leaders purblind as the kings of our tale.

A war is launched; the fates move close. "What goes around" is ruthless, mindless. "What comes around" is, for the present, unknown, ominous. It is also biblically inevitable. We shall pay in the coin we have traded in. The prophets summon us to judgment.

~

Another resemblance of the American empire to the era of Kings: today too the gods of war are obsessively invoked. Those who claim whatever favoring god ignore peace-making Christ and his urging: that we take his task for our own.

We ponder his words and behavior. What we find in the Gospels is hardly reassuring: a strict repudiation of the wars of the Hebrew bible. No word indicates admiration or empathy for the violence of Saul, David, Solomon, Hezekiah, and the others. Jesus never draws on them, even by way of rebuttal, to enlarge or illustrate his teaching. The contempt, the silence are deafening.

In place of the kings, images of the prophets loom large. In the synagogue of Nazareth, through the words of Isaiah, Christ conveys the substance of his vocation. Works of mercy and mitigation will mark his days: "Good news to the poor, release to captives, sight to the blind, liberty for the oppressed . . ."

~

Wartime, and a question. Does war alter our "grammar of assent"?

In times of peace, do we see ourselves as Christians (a solid, sure noun) who happen to be American (adjective, of secondary import)? Which is to suggest: we could be Christians who "happen to be" Afghan or Iraqi. An alteration in our self-understanding, to be sure; but the center and pivot, "Christian," would stand firm, the task and blessing accorded to peacemakers. And this, whether we live amid victims or victimizers: small matter, same vocation.

Wartime. And we are subtly or overtly urged: Alter the sense of who you are in the world. Lines are drawn; the culture of war exerts a huge, central claim. The cultural enlistment is a curse; we are urged to ignore the central teaching and example of Christ. "For the duration," we are to be Americans first and foremost — Americans who happen to be Christians.

~

One must urge (to his own soul first) a firm rebutting midrash; bring Christ to bear. Read the gospel closely, obediently. Welcome no enticements, no other claim on conscience. Mourn the preachers and priests whose silence and collusion signal plain revolt against the gospel. Enter the maelstrom, the wilderness; flee the claim that would possess your soul. Earn the blessing; pay up.

Wartime horrors — perpetual, perennial.

Nonetheless. Blessed — and lonely and powerless and intent on the Master — and, if must be, despised, scorned, locked up — blessed are the makers of peace.